PIML

615

THE BEATLES AT NO. 1

Ian MacDonald was born in 1948. A writer with many interests, he was Assistant Editor of the *New Musical Express* during 1972–5. He also worked as a songwriter and record producer, and is the author of *The New Shostakovich* (1990), the acclaimed *Revolution in the Head: The Beatles' Records and the Sixties* (1994, revised 1997) and, most recently, *The People's Music* (2003). He died in August 2003.

THE BEATLES AT NO. 1

IAN MacDONALD

PIMLICO

This book consists of selected extracts from Ian MacDonald's
Revolution in the Head: The Beatles' Music and the Sixties
(revised edition, Pimlico 1998), with a new introduction by the author

Published by Pimlico 2003

2 4 6 8 10 9 7 5 3 1

First published in Great Britain by
Pimlico 2003

Pimlico
Random House, 20 Vauxhall Bridge Road,
London SW1V 2SA

Random House Australia (Pty) Limited
20 Alfred Street, Milsons Point, Sydney,
New South Wales 2061, Australia

Random House New Zealand Limited
18 Poland Road, Glenfield,
Auckland 10, New Zealand

Random House (Pty) Limited
Endulini, 5A Jubilee Road, Parktown 2193, South Africa

The Random House Group Limited Reg. No. 954009
www.randomhouse.co.uk

A CIP catalogue record for this book
is available from the British Library

ISBN 1-8441-3429-6

Papers used by Random House are natural,
recyclable products made from wood grown in sustainable forests;
the manufacturing processes conform to the environmental
regulations of the country of origin

Printed and bound in Great Britain by
Bookmarque Ltd, Croydon, Surrey

Contents

Introduction

The Beatles' stellar career, which ran for a little over seven years, coincided with a remarkable flowering of pop music on both sides of the Atlantic. Year on year from 1963, the scene in general improved in inspiration, sophistication, and sheer quality, an ascending trajectory likewise traceable in The Beatles' succession of No. 1 singles during that period. Arguably the arc peaked in 1966, thereafter beginning a long, slow decline which has continued in successive decades (and which can be detected in The Beatles later No. 1 singles). In other words, The Beatles' music waxed and waned in synchronisation with the rest of pop music in their time. To listen to their twenty-seven No. 1s is to witness, by representation, the rise and incipient slow fall of popular music as a whole in the Sixties and thereafter.

LOVE ME DO, issued as The Beatles first UK single on Parlophone in October 1962, reached No. 1 in the USA in May 1964 in the aftermath of the group's epoch-making appearance on *The Ed Sullivan Show*. An almost skeletally simple song, it has about it the plainness of the pop music of its time. A hesitant entry on the path to fame, it reflects a scene idling before the great swooping take-off into the heady years of the mid-Sixties. Society then was still monochromatic and strait-laced; the colour and freedom brought in by the generational upheaval of that decade were yet to be summoned up; the excitement and sense of acceleration which were to come are scarcely present in this record, which holds its retrospective eminence chiefly by virtue of its historic significance.

FROM ME TO YOU, The Beatles third UK single and first UK No. 1 (in April 1963), is noticeably more animated. There's something new going on here, a sense that pop music is beginning to move ahead into an unpredictable but promising future. SHE LOVES YOU, by contrast, is pellmell exhilaration, a clear token of the impending ascendancy of an entirely fresh sort of inspiration in which new forms and feelings were about to become the stamp of both The Beatles' music and of pop music as a whole. Reaching No. 1 in the UK in August 1963, SHE LOVES YOU became the best-selling UK single of all time until 1977. In America, it was the group's second No. 1 after their breakthrough record I WANT TO HOLD YOUR HAND, reaching the top of the chart in February 1964. But it was I WANT TO HOLD YOUR HAND, The Beatles' third UK No. 1 in December 1963, which, in January 1964, broke the group in the USA. There, The Beatles' first American No. 1 had a youthquake impact which remains in the realm of legend, convulsing the American pop music scene and inaugurating the unprecedented upsurge of popularity of all kinds of UK pop which became known as 'the British Invasion', a phenomenon which continued for the next two years.

CAN'T BUY ME LOVE, The Beatles' fourth UK No. 1 and third US No. 1 in March 1964, is the record which confirmed their arrival at the summit of pop music on both sides of the Atlantic. A McCartney song (unlike the Lennon and McCartney collaborations which had featured previously among the group's singles), CAN'T BUY ME LOVE is a buoyantly jazzy variation on the blues which spoke alike to young and old listeners, establishing The Beatles' unique cross-generational appeal. A HARD DAY'S NIGHT, which provided the group with their fifth No. 1 singles in the UK and the USA in July 1964, heralded the film of the same name which caught the essence of British Beatlemania in a comic rush of bantering wit, excitement, and energy. Shot in black and white, *A Hard Day's Night* was the epitome of the early Sixties pop impulse. Colour was about to burst on the cinematic scene as if for the first time, bidden by the new thrilling current now pulsing through pop music in both Britain and America.

Becoming The Beatles' sixth No. 1 single in both the UK and USA in December 1964, the joyous I FEEL FINE was, like A HARD DAY'S NIGHT, a Lennon song. It was followed, in the USA but not in the UK, by EIGHT DAYS A WEEK, a Lennon and McCartney collaboration which soared to the top of the American chart in February 1965. This pealingly jubilant inspiration was followed by two Lennon songs, TICKET TO RIDE and HELP!, No. 1s in April and July 1965 respectively. Both records saw a deepening of mood and expression partly attributable to The Beatles' espousal of cannabis as an aid to creation. In particular, TICKET TO RIDE, with its clangorous wall-of-sound approach, pointed to the coming into being of a new, heavier, more generally sense-oriented style which would soon be dubbed simply 'rock'.

Like EIGHT DAYS A WEEK, YESTERDAY, The Beatles' tenth American No. 1, was never released as a single in the UK. Here, in October 1965, McCartney's acoustic inspiration, linked with a string quartet, broke new ground in pop music, setting a regretfully yearning song in a chastely understated classical context which would soon find echoes all over the scene (and especially in the passing sub-genre known as 'baroque rock'). DAY TRIPPER and WE CAN WORK IT OUT, a pioneering 'double A-side' single which registered two more No. 1s for The Beatles in December 1965, heralded their middle period, built around the albums *Revolver* (August 1966) and *Sergeant Pepper's Lonely Hearts Club Band* (June 1967). Both songs were fifty-fifty collaborations by Lennon and McCartney, WE CAN WORK IT OUT being one of the most effective expressions of the contrast in their ways of composing and a key record in the short-lived idiom of 'folk rock'.

The Beatles' middle period, which more or less coincides with the peak years of pop, 1965–7, was inaugurated, so far as their haul of No. 1 singles is concerned, by PAPERBACK WRITER in June 1966. This eruptive McCartney number, with its Swinging London undertones, was the group's tenth UK chart-topper and the twelfth of their singles to conquer America. ELEANOR RIGBY/YELLOW SUBMARINE, another double A-side of McCartney songs, this time taken from *Revolver*, was listed as two No. 1 hits in the UK, but was awarded separate chart placings in America, resulting in neither side making the top of the stateside chart. Here, the new textural and expressive complexity of The Beatles' work coincided with yet another upward step in creativity for pop music in general. Now the group was including among its sources of inspiration the powerful hallucinogenic drug LSD. 'Acid rock' would soon take over as the idiom of the time, its visionary illuminations spilling over the hitherto standard three-minute limit of most pop music and sometimes inhabiting entire sides of albums, which suddenly became as important a medium as chart singles.

Continuing The Beatles' new vein of sonic and imaginative experimentation, PENNY LANE/STRAWBERRY FIELDS FOREVER, yet another double A-side, notoriously failed to make it higher than No. 2 in the UK, though PENNY LANE, listed separately in the USA, did peak at No. 1 in March 1967, the group's thirteenth American chart-topper. Perhaps The Beatles' most perfect middle-period pop single, McCartney's PENNY LANE abounded with a confidence and vigour which faithfully expressed the group's awareness of being at the summit of their inspiration (and perhaps at the all-time peak of pop music).

Lennon's ALL YOU NEED IS LOVE, their fourteenth US and twelfth UK No. 1 in July 1967, shows The Beatles beginning to idle, marking time with an easygoing anthem to the year's sunny 'Summer of Love' and the hippie counterculture which had sprung up on both sides of the Atlantic during the previous eighteen months.

McCartney's HELLO, GOODBYE, a No. 1 in both Britain and America in December 1967, continued the subtle levelling-off of The Beatles' inspiration, offering nursery rhyme aesthetics in place of something more forward-reaching. At the same time, pop music in general began likewise to flatten and dip in its creative trajectory. LADY MADONNA, another McCartney song, embraced a back-to-rock'n'roll shift to more simplified and direct expression. No. 1 in Britain in March 1968, it climbed only as high as No. 4 in the States. Yet another McCartney effort, the stately HEY JUDE became the summer anthem of its year in September 1968, released on The Beatles' own Apple label and registering as their fifteenth British and sixteenth American No. 1s. Continuing his run of Beatles A-sides, McCartney contributed the decidedly rootsy GET BACK in 1969, reaching No. 1 in the UK in April and in the USA in May.

THE BALLAD OF JOHN AND YOKO, Lennon's almost rudi-

mentary rocker – expressly autobiographical and realised
with the help of McCartney alone in the studio – made
No. 1 in the UK in June 1969, climbing only to No. 8
in America. By now, The Beatles were almost spent as
a creative force. Their next No. 1, the double A-side
SOMETHING/COME TOGETHER (by Harrison and Lennon
respectively), failed to make the top of the UK chart but
constituted the group's eighteenth and nineteenth US
No. 1s. McCartney's hymnic LET IT BE rose only to No.
2 in Britain, but gave The Beatles their twentieth
American No. 1 in March 1970. THE LONG AND WINDING
ROAD, another McCartney ballad, was never released as
a single in the UK, but became the group's twenty-first
and final No. 1 in the USA in May 1970.

The fact that The Beatles' talent waxed and waned in
rhythm with the entire contemporary pop scene is a
token of how closely they embody the spirit and character of their time. Even a group as outstandingly gifted
as The Beatles were part of their age and subject to its
fluctuations and novelties. Thus, when one listens to
their No. 1s in chronological order, one hears a social
narrative of the Sixties in musical form. These twenty-
seven records tell us of an extraordinary epoch in which,
for a while, things could only get better – and at dizzying

speed. The Beatles and the Sixties are inextricably linked with each other. Rarely has popular music spoken so vividly and resonantly of its time.

Ian MacDonald

1 **Love Me Do** (*McCartney–Lennon*)

McCartney vocal, bass; **Lennon** vocal, harmonica, rhythm guitar (?); **Harrison** acoustic rhythm guitar, backing vocal; **Starr** drums (version 1); tambourine (version 2); **Andy White** drums (version 2).
Recorded: 6 June, 4, 11 September 1962, Abbey Road 2.
Producer: George Martin. Engineer: Norman Smith.
UK release: 5 October 1962 (A single/P.S. I Love You).
US release: 27 April 1964 (A single/P.S. I Love You).

Made up while 'sagging off' (playing truant) from the Liverpool Institute in 1958, Love Me Do was one of 16-year-old Paul McCartney's earliest songs. Unsure of how to finish it, he showed it to his friend John Lennon, who may have contributed the rudimentary middle eight. The lyric is perfunctory and, where pop numbers of this period classically revolved around three common chords, Love Me Do mostly makes do with two (G and C).

One of half a dozen songs rehearsed during the afternoon of 4 September 1962 in Abbey Road's Studio 3,

LOVE ME DO had to wait on Parlophone's preferred choice HOW DO YOU DO IT? before being attempted by an understandably jittery group. (Unused to headphones, they were stiff with nerves and took fifteen takes to get it right.) Both songs were considered for release as The Beatles' debut single but, during the two hours it had taken to make, George Martin had formed a hunch about LOVE ME DO. Its vernacular title, dockside harmonica, and open harmonies had a freshness that suited the group and seemed intriguingly hard to categorise. Texan singer Bruce Channel's plaintive 'Hey! Baby', a hit in Britain that spring, had featured similar harmonica but, apart from that, nothing else on the market sounded anything like it.

There was still, though, something bothering him about LOVE ME DO: Starr's drumming. (The legend is that he was unsteady, hurrying into the choruses.) According to Abbey Road's general manager Ken Townsend, McCartney was as dissatisfied as Martin with Starr's approach, though when questioned by Mark Lewisohn twenty-five years later the song's author put a different spin on it. Martin, he recalled, decided that LOVE ME DO needed remaking with a session drummer because Starr had failed to 'lock in' his bass-drum with the bass guitar. This convention of the polite studio style of the early Sixties was about to vanish under the impact of loose-swinging drummers like Starr and The Rolling Stones' Charlie Watts (to reappear around 1980 under the automated auspices of the drum-machine). However, in 1962 Starr's virtue as an intuitive time-keeper had yet to be recognised and consequently the group trooped back into Studio 2 a week later to record LOVE ME DO all over again. Andy White, a regular player on EMI sessions, 'sat in' on drums while a disenchanted Starr tapped a superfluous reinforcement to the snare on tambourine. In the event, both versions of LOVE ME DO were issued: the first (mixed bottom-light to disguise Starr's bass-drum) went out as the A-side of The Beatles' first single; the second was issued on later versions of the single and as the opening track on Side 2 of the group's debut album *Please Please Me*.

Written in what the group thought of as a 'bluesy' style, LOVE ME DO was extraordinarily raw by the standards of its time, standing out from the tame fare offered on the Light Programme and Radio Luxembourg like a bare brick wall in a suburban sitting-room. Indeed, next to the standard pop output then strolling blandly up and

down the 'hit parade' on Alan Freeman's *Pick of the Pops*
every Sunday, its modal gauntness seemed almost primitive. As such, the public were puzzled by it and sales
were cautious. While the record's erratic progress to its
highest position at No. 17 in December was followed
with excitement by Beatle fans in Liverpool, many
thought it a poor advertisement for the energy the group
generated live. Purists claimed, too, that the arrangement had been messed about with. George Martin had
changed the solo vocal line crossing into the harmonica
break, giving it to McCartney instead of Lennon on the
grounds that, due to an overlap between the last word
and the first harmonica note, the latter had been singing
'Love me *waahh!*', which was deemed uncommercial.
(According to McCartney, they hadn't rehearsed with
the harmonica and had to alter the arrangement on the
spot under Martin's direction.)

Simple as it is, LOVE ME DO was quite a cunning
record, serving to introduce The Beatles to the English
public in several ways at once. As rearranged under
Martin's direction, it offered two features for the leaders
(Lennon's harmonica riff, McCartney's unaccompanied
title-phrase) as well as its playground-appeal 'hook' (the
drone-harmonised 'Ple-e-e-ease') and a little character

spot for Starr (his po-faced cymbal crash at the end of Lennon's solo). Only Harrison stayed in the background, strumming diffidently. But the subtlest effect was the record's air of unvarnished honesty. Though the stark, open-fifth vocal harmony was bathed in reverb, the rest of the production was startlingly 'dry' compared with the echo-saturated sound of UK pop during the preceding four years. The result was a candour which perfectly complemented the group's forthright image, setting them apart from everything else on offer.

If one element of the record can be said to have counted above all others it was Lennon's wailing harmonica. Played with passionate overblowing and no 'bent' notes, it had little in common with any of the American blues styles, instead suggesting to British audiences the blunt vitality of working-class Northernness as introduced around 1960 in the sound-tracks to films like *Room at the Top, Saturday Night and Sunday Morning*, and *A Taste of Honey*.

Many UK pop musicians have since recalled sensing something epochal in LOVE ME DO when it first appeared. Crude as it was compared to The Beatles' later achievements, it blew a stimulating autumn breeze through an enervated pop scene, heralding a change in the tone of post-war British life matched by the contemporary appearances of the first James Bond film, *Dr No*, and BBC TV's live satirical programme *That Was The Week That Was*. From now on, social influence in Britain was to swing away from the old class-based order of deference to 'elders and betters' and succumb to the frank and fearless energy of 'the younger generation'. The first faint chime of a revolutionary bell, LOVE ME DO represented far more than the sum of its simple parts. A new spirit was abroad: artless yet unabashed – and awed by nothing.

2 **From Me To You**
(McCartney–Lennon)

Lennon vocal, rhythm guitar, harmonica; **McCartney**
vocal, bass; **Harrison** harmony vocal, lead guitar; **Starr**
drums.
  Recorded: 5 March 1963, Abbey Road 2.
  Producer: George Martin. Engineer: Norman Smith.
  UK release: 11 April 1963 (A single/THANK YOU GIRL).
  US release: 27 May 1963 (A single/THANK YOU GIRL).

Though Lennon and McCartney wrote a substantial
number of songs between 1957 and 1962, their confidence in all but a few of them was low. The majority of
the group's pre-1963 act consisted of other people's
material with only an apologetic leavening of
Lennon–McCartney originals. Realising the weakness of
his protégés' existing catalogue, George Martin advised
them to come up with more hits without delay, a plea
repeated with added urgency when PLEASE PLEASE ME
began to move in large quantities. They wasted little

time. Based on the letters page of *New Musical Express* ('From You To Us'), FROM ME TO YOU was written on the Helen Shapiro tour bus on 28 February 1963 – the group's first custom-built Beatles song as Parlophone artists.

Dismissed in most accounts of their career as a transitional time-marker between PLEASE PLEASE ME and [3] SHE LOVES YOU, FROM ME TO YOU was actually a brilliant consolidation of the emerging Beatles sound, holding the No. 1 position for seven weeks (the longest occupation of this place by any of their eighteen British No. 1 singles apart from [19] HELLO, GOODBYE and [22] GET BACK). That it was specifically designed to accomplish this testifies to the canny practicality of the group's songwriting duo. Like most of Lennon and McCartney's few recorded full fifty-fifty collaborations, FROM ME TO YOU proceeds in the two-bar phrases a pair of writers typically adopt when tentatively ad-libbing at each other. The usual result of such a synthetic process, in which neither contributor is free to develop the melody-line in his normal way, is a competition to produce surprising developments of the initial idea. As in [4] I WANT TO HOLD YOUR HAND, the variation surprise in FROM ME TO YOU consists of a sudden falsetto octave leap, a motif first tried on the chorus of PLEASE PLEASE ME (itself rewritten in this to-and-fro fashion).

Bluesily horizontal in its intervals, FROM ME TO YOU clearly grew from an original Lennon phrase, perhaps passing to McCartney for the vertical second phrase (delivered by Lennon with a rasping upward slide into falsetto, harmonised by his partner a pleading third below). The New York quartet The Four Seasons, then climbing the UK charts with 'Big Girls Don't Cry', employed similar falsetto and almost certainly influenced The Beatles in this respect. Yet where the Americans built falsetto into their four-part harmony, The Beatles wielded it as an isolated device, and it was mainly these sudden hair-raising wails that made their early records so rivetingly strange. Far from a clever novelty, however, FROM ME TO YOU has a distinctive mood of its own, Lennon's abrasive voice – the trademark of the group's 'Beatlemania' phase – turning a trite lyric into something mordantly sardonic. His harmonica, insisted on by George Martin, maintains continuity with the group's first two singles, adding to the wildness so crucial to The Beatles' early impact. (At the peak of the second middle eight, the brew bubbles over as McCartney's ascending harmony meets Lennon's octave-jumping lead above an augmented seventh and a typically idiosyncratic 'backwards' fill from Starr.)

FROM ME TO YOU demonstrates The Beatles' pop professionalism, only the functionality of McCartney's bass part betraying that less than a week had elapsed between writing and recording it. Echoing the wit they were displaying in their TV and radio interviews, their deftness and adaptability in the studio was already far beyond the reach of their immediate competitors.

By now, it was clear that something unprecedented and unpredictable was happening and, as the song raced to the top of the UK singles chart during the summer of 1963, a change could be felt in the atmosphere of English life. With sex newly an acceptable social topic courtesy of Vassall, Ward, Keeler and James Bond, the frank physicality of The Beatles' music – epitomised by Lennon's mocking leer, lazy strum and open-legged stance at the microphone – had arrived at exactly the right time. As the nation's centre of gravity slid from upper lip to lower hip, a degree of Dionysiac abandon was only to be expected, yet the shrill gales of ululation which began to greet the announcement of the group's names before their live appearances took even The Beatles by surprise. Girls had been squirming about and screaming at their pop idols since Presley first pumped his pelvis at them in 1956, but what was happening now was mass hysteria. Jess Conrad, a typical 'teen idol' of the period, recalls appearing with the group on a pop show around this time: 'I did my record and the girls went crazy as usual – but when The Beatles went on the place exploded! I thought "These boys really have it".' This orgiastic release of erotic energy dammed up during the repressive Fifties – a ceaseless avian shrilling so loud that the bands, standing only yards away from their amplifiers, could barely hear what they were playing – was soon greeting every 'beat' group to bob up in The Beatles' wake.

3 **She Loves You** (*Lennon–McCartney*)

Lennon vocal, rhythm guitar; **McCartney** vocal, bass;
Harrison harmony vocal, lead guitar; **Starr** drums.
Recorded: 1 July 1963, Abbey Road 2.
 Producer: George Martin. Engineer: Norman Smith.
 UK release: 23 August 1963 (A single/I'LL GET YOU).
 US release: 16 September 1963 (A single/I'LL GET YOU).

Lennon and McCartney wrote SHE LOVES YOU in a
Newcastle hotel room after a gig at the Majestic Ballroom
on 26 June 1963. The initial idea (from McCartney)
consisted of using the third person rather than their
usual first and second. To judge from the expressive link
between the song's words and melody, a roughed-out
lyric must have come next, after which the pair presumably fell into the phrase-swapping mode familiar from
[2] FROM ME TO YOU.

 The opening lines follow speech inflections and stay
within the compass of their chords – obviously Lennon's
work. What changes them, making a straightforward

sequence surprising, is McCartney's harmony. Already maturing, the partnership's writing formula can be heard here as the dual expression of Lennon's downbeat cynicism and McCartney's get-up-and-go optimism. Much of the pair's musical originality derived from their self-taught willingness to let their fingers discover chord sequences by exploring the architecture of their guitars rather than following orthodox progressions. Yet these choices were driven by the harmonies they used – and these arguably reflected the contrast of their temperaments. Even at this stage their relationship could be acerbic and they were capable of bickering vitriolically in public, though under this lay an enduring emotional bond and a steady respect for each other's talent and intelligence which overrode their disagreements. Like all lasting music, The Beatles' best work is as much the expression of a state of mind as a construction in sound, and in SHE LOVES YOU Lennon and McCartney can be heard fusing their different outlooks in musical form. The result is an authentic distillation of the atmosphere of that time, and one of the most explosive pop records ever made.

Five days after writing the song, they were in Studio 2 at Abbey Road, giving it final shape. Beyond the basic words and music lay the vital work of arranging, at which juncture The Beatles became not a duo but a quartet. The contribution of Starr and Harrison to SHE LOVES YOU demonstrates the group's acute cohesion. The drums on the chorus – which, reputedly on George Martin's advice, begins the song, delaying arrival at the tonic (G major) – are intrinsic to the track's dynamics, creating tension by replacing the offbeat with tom-tom quavers before blazing into the thrashed open hi-hat of Starr's classic-Beatlemania style. Steering the arrangement's changes with his gruff seven-note riff and gleaming Gretsch arpeggios, Harrison completes his contribution by adding a jazz sixth to the final 'Yeah' of the chorus. No record of the takes involved in making SHE LOVES YOU survives and it is impossible to know how much of its final form was evolved during the five-hour session in which it and its B-side, I'LL GET YOU, were recorded. The Beatles were known for their agility in making adjustments from take to take, and Johnny Dean, editor of *The Beatles Book*, who was at the session, recalls that the song seemed to him to have altered quite dramatically by the time it reached the form preserved on record. If so, that only serves as further testament to the tightness of The Beatles as an operating unit. There were no passengers in this group and, when a situation warranted it, their drive to achieve was unanimous.

Issued in Britain in August 1963, SHE LOVES YOU was an enormous hit and remains their biggest-selling UK single. Prodigally original yet instantly communicative, it owed much of its success to the naturalness of the match between its music and the everyday language of its lyric. The contour of the melodic line fits the feeling and rhythm of the words perfectly – and, where it doesn't, the singers make a virtue out of it by altering their inflection (e.g., the cajoling emphasis of 'apologise to her'). Indeed, so much were Lennon and McCartney led by their lyric conception here that there was no room for their usual middle eight, the space being usurped by an outrageous eight-bar bridge which, via a violent push, lands on C minor. Beyond doubt, though, the record's hottest attraction was its notorious 'Yeah, yeah, yeah' refrain, from which the group became known throughout Europe as The Yeah-Yeahs. (Almost as celebrated were their falsetto 'ooo's, stolen from The Isley Brothers' 'Twist And Shout' and grafted onto SHE LOVES YOU, along with the visual hook of McCartney and Harrison shaking their mop-top hair-dos as they delivered them. When The Beatles first showed this to their colleagues on tour, it was greeted with hilarity. Lennon, though, insisted that it would work, and was proved correct. Whenever the head-shaking 'ooo's came round, the level of the audiences' delirium would leap.)

Claiming the British showbiz throne with their appearance on ITV's *Sunday Night At The London Palladium* on 13 October, the group brought their set to a climax with SHE LOVES YOU. For the first time, a pop phenomenon which thrilled the country's youngsters became ruefully acknowledged by their parents. Overnight, Britain took The Beatles to its heart. (And enter the calculatingly offensive Rolling Stones.) Meanwhile, America remained immune, Capitol again refusing a release. When Vee Jay too backed out, a desperate Epstein licensed SHE LOVES YOU to Swan Records of Philadelphia, yet the compilers of US radio playlists showed no interest.

4 I Want To Hold Your Hand
(Lennon–McCartney)

Lennon vocal, rhythm guitar, handclaps; **McCartney** vocal, bass, handclaps; **Harrison** harmony vocal, lead guitar, handclaps; **Starr** drums, handclaps
Recorded: 17 October 1963, Abbey Road 2.
Producer: George Martin. Engineer: Norman Smith.
UK release: 29 November 1963 (A single/THIS BOY).
US release: 26 December 1963 (A single/I SAW HER STANDING THERE).

With [3] SHE LOVES YOU at No. 1 in the UK throughout September, The Beatles took their second holiday since signing with EMI, returning to Britain early in October. During this break Lennon and McCartney wrote the two sides of their next single, the first Beatles songs for nearly a year not to have been dashed off while touring. Capitol's refusal to issue the band's product in the USA was by now an impediment to their career and a major worry to Brian Epstein who advised the pair to write with

America in mind. Knowing they were on their mettle induced a tension tangible in the introduction of the song they came up with: I WANT TO HOLD YOUR HAND.

Written ('one on one, eyeball to eyeball', according to Lennon) in the basement of Jane Asher's parents' house in Wimpole Street, I WANT TO HOLD YOUR HAND displays the traits of the early Lennon–McCartney collaborative style. Going above all for impact, it makes no attempt at sustained melody, moving instead in half-bar phrases governed by its fourth-dominated harmony, the result of two writers competing with each other side by side at the same piano. As with PLEASE PLEASE ME and [2] FROM ME TO YOU, the method depended on surprise; indeed, the song is so dense with incident that McCartney's octave jump to falsetto at the end of the verse is pre-empted by another shock four bars earlier: a plunge from the home key of G major onto an unstable B minor. Such blatant contrivance mattered no more than it had in PLEASE PLEASE ME. It was exciting, unexpected, irreverent – and in practice made to seem natural by the beatific vitality with which the group belted it out.

Brought into the studio four days after the press had announced the onset of Beatlemania following the group's appearance on *Sunday Night At The London*

Palladium, I WANT TO HOLD YOUR HAND was thoroughly prearranged and rehearsed, only the eleven-bar middle section being altered on take 2, dropping Lennon's rock-and-roll rhythm figure for the contrast of quiet arpeggios. The introduction postponed arrival at the tonic by starting with the last bars of the middle section. This time, though, the device was intensified with hammering repetition and a 'pushed' beat which created ambiguity in the rhythm, compounded by having the vocals enter two beats ahead of the verse ('*Oh yeah*, I . . .'). To complete this barrage of dazzling effects, the group brought the performance to a breathless full close on two bars of hard-braking 3/8. Apart from ending with the studio exploding, they could scarcely have hit their prospective American audience with more in two and a half minutes.

In the UK, I WANT TO HOLD YOUR HAND was The Beatles' first Christmas hit, entering the shops in late November with advance orders of more than a million. In the USA, release came too late for the festive season which, in any case, had been dampened by the recent assassination of President Kennedy. When Capitol finally capitulated to Epstein's pressure and issued I WANT TO HOLD YOUR HAND, the record's joyous energy and invention lifted America out of its gloom, following which, high on gratitude, the country cast itself at The Beatles' feet. Their TV performance on *The Ed Sullivan Show* on 9 February, claimed by many US commentators to be the pivotal event in American post-war culture, sealed the deal and, by April, their back catalogue was flooding the US charts.

I WANT TO HOLD YOUR HAND electrified American pop. More schooled in technique than their British cousins, aspiring American players and writers listened to The Beatles' free-spirited unorthodoxies in excited disbelief. Just as Lennon, McCartney and Harrison had studied the licks, changes and production-effects used in the rock-and-roll and R&B records they had once bought at Liverpool import shops, so now American youths crouched by their dansettes with guitars trying to work out what The Beatles were doing. Most of the North American groups of the late Sixties acknowledged the inspiration of The Beatles and their role in breaking the grip of showbiz convention on the US pop industry. In fact, every American artist, black or white, asked about I WANT TO HOLD YOUR HAND has said much the same: it altered everything, ushering in a new era and changing their lives. That The Beatles represented something transmitting at a higher creative frequency was clear even to many outside the pop audience. The poet Allen Ginsberg, for example, amazed his intellectual *confrères* by getting up and dancing delightedly to I WANT TO HOLD YOUR HAND when he first heard it in a New York nightclub. Bob Dylan, too, was able to see past the song's naivety to the epoch-making spirit animating it. (Fascinated by The Beatles' unorthodox chords and harmonies, he decided they must have been chemically assisted, mishearing the line 'I can't hide' as 'I get high'.)

Not that The Beatles were uniformly welcomed in the USA. The upmarket press was notably sniffy, finding the group's music barbarous and their lyrics illiterate, while the existing pop industry naturally resented the prospect of overnight obsolescence. (In moves to avoid this, many established artists made floundering attempts to adjust their styles to meet the 'British Invasion' of lesser UK acts that soon poured in following The Beatles' break-through.) Some of the adverse reaction was justified. Tommy James, a pop star with an interest in production, thought much of the early Beatles repertoire poorly recorded – which, by US standards, it was. While I WANT TO HOLD YOUR HAND (the first Beatles song to be made in true stereo on Abbey Road's new four-track desk) sounded better than most of the group's previous discs, it was primitive compared with the product of American studios, lacking bass response and offering raw vocal sound. What it did have, apart from power and originality, was an instinct for dynamic contrast and a brilliant grasp of construction.

Primarily a hit *record*, I WANT TO HOLD YOUR HAND makes less sense considered as a song. So much of its melody line is disguised harmony that singing it without chordal support makes for comic results, while its lyrics are embarrassingly perfunctory. In America, the words to I WANT TO HOLD YOUR HAND were heard as a token of the group's social acceptability. Where The Rolling Stones dealt in sex, The Beatles supposedly respected propriety, knowing how far a young man should go with a young woman and hence how far a pop group could trespass without causing offence. This was true to the extent that Brian Epstein had carefully sweetened The Beatles' image for public consumption (much to the rebellious Lennon's annoyance).

Yet the real reason for the group's lyric blandness at this stage was that they didn't much care what words they sang as long as they fitted the overall sound. It was the record, rather than the song, that interested them.

Haunted by the often imponderably strange productions that emerged from US studios during the Fifties – 'Give Me Love' by Rosie and The Originals being one of their favourites – McCartney and (particularly) Lennon were more devoted to spirit than form. To them, the sound and feel of a record mattered more than what it literally said; hence, the first requirement of a lyric was not to get in the way of the general effect. The Beatles sang of 'diamond rings' in their early songs not because they wished to identify themselves with the marital conventions of the silent majority, but because it then seemed to them that clichés were less distracting than anything more original.

The epochal change that American listeners sensed in I WANT TO HOLD YOUR HAND was, in fact, nothing less than a resumption, at higher intensity, of the carefree sensationalism of Fifties rock'n'roll. Since Little Richard's crazed clarion call of 'Awopbopaloomop, alop-bamboom!', pop had strayed only timidly from the straight and narrow of civilised 'good sense'. Indeed, the American folk-protest movement had thrust plain-speaking so obtrusively into the pop domain that every transient youth idol was then routinely interrogated concerning his or her 'message' to humanity. If it has any message at all, that of I WANT TO HOLD YOUR HAND is 'Let go – *feel how good it is*'. This though (as conservative commentators knew very well) implied a fundamental break with the Christian bourgeois status quo. Harbouring no conscious subversive intent, The Beatles, with this potent record, perpetrated a culturally revolutionary act. As the decade wore on and they began to realise the position they were in, they began to do the same thing more deliberately.

5 Can't Buy Me Love
(Lennon–McCartney)

McCartney double-tracked vocal, bass; **Lennon** acoustic rhythm guitar; **Harrison** double-tracked lead guitar; **Starr** drums.

Recorded: 29 January 1964, EMI Pathé Marconi, Paris; 25th February 1964, Abbey Road 2.

Producer: George Martin. Engineer: Norman Smith.

UK release: 20 March 1964 (A single/YOU CAN'T DO THAT).

US release: 16 March 1964 (A single/YOU CAN'T DO THAT).

The Beatles' January 1964 residency at the Paris Olympia was a chore, their audiences finding the new British pop idiom hard to grasp and the French press loftily insulting the group as 'juvenile delinquents' and 'has-beens'. While their spirits were raised by hearing that [4] I WANT TO HOLD YOUR HAND had vaulted in virtually one bound to the top of the American charts, more drudgery had to be faced on 29 January when they reluctantly attended EMI France's Paris studio to tape German-language versions of it and [3] SHE LOVES YOU. These done, they used the last hour of the session to record a number McCartney had written only days before. Originally conceived with the rolling backbeat and bluesy delivery later used in SHE'S A WOMAN, CAN'T BUY ME LOVE was altered on the spot, turning into a bouncily commerical pop song – a redraft accomplished in four takes. The fact that George Martin had to tell the group to start with the chorus rather than the verse shows how little they'd considered the song before recording it (the change being so obvious that they would have made it themselves had they tried the tune out earlier).

Among the simplest of the group's hits, CAN'T BUY ME LOVE consists of a jazzy blues in minor chords with a straight-up eight-bar major chorus. As such, it spoke a musical language the parental generation could relate to, and it was almost logical that Ella Fitzgerald recorded a cover version as soon as she heard it. The only incongruity lay in McCartney's artless lyric which, despite some smart syllabics in the second line of its second verse, stands no comparison with the work of the professional lyricists to whom Fitzgerald was accustomed. The most effective aspect of the words to CAN'T BUY ME LOVE was largely accidental: its author's decision to replace the conventional 'my dear/my love' with the bluff, asexual 'my friend'. Though McCartney was merely recycling a throwaway rhyme from the little-known I'LL GET YOU, the effect was arresting, seeming to define the casual etiquette of a coolly unromantic new age.

Partly by luck, partly by intuition, The Beatles managed time and again with such simple strokes to place themselves in a subtly futuristic context. As the decade advanced and they continued to bring off variations on this trick, a sense grew among their audience that the group 'knew what was going on' and were somehow poised above events, guiding them through their music. Yet The Beatles wooed convention with an equally intuitive touch, establishing their cross-generational viability in America with CAN'T BUY ME LOVE in the aftermath of the youthquake impact of I WANT TO HOLD YOUR HAND. Where the latter threatened something almost too vigorous to be contained, the idiomatic familiarity of CAN'T BUY ME LOVE, delivered with old-fashioned showbiz 'oomph' by the wholesome McCartney, offered canny reassurance – a sly conquest soon consolidated by the cheeky wit of *A Hard Day's Night*.

The Beatles' ability to be two contradictory things at once – comfortably safe and exhilaratingly strange – has been displayed by no other pop act. A by-product of the creative tension between the group's two dominant personalities, this effect increased as Lennon and McCartney drew apart as writers, and it is significant that, with CAN'T BUY ME LOVE, their 'one on one, eyeball to eyeball' collaborations more or less came to an end. So far as records are concerned, the pair's golden age of full fifty-fifty co-composition was 1963, with a sustained run of such numbers. Only one such occurred in 1964 and the same was true in 1965. During The Beatles' last four years, Lennon and McCartney stopped working together like this, though they continued to meet formally to 'check' each other's new songs in three-hour writing sessions held mostly at Lennon's house in Weybridge. Here, they would show each other their new material, fixing details and often helping with unfinished or unwritten sections, such as middle eights. Several of their best tracks resulted from semi-collaborations begun after one of them had written part of a number and needed help from the other with finishing it. So far as songwriting was concerned, Lennon and McCartney saw themselves as business partners and took a disciplined professional attitude to their work. Yet the truth was that each was a self-sufficient entity with an egotistic eye on his own career and a different conception of the group. Similar enough to allow fruitful interaction in the later stages of composition, their tastes in music, as they grew up, diverged too much to accommodate much full-scale start-to-finish collaboration. Theirs was a classic attraction of opposites, and one which worked increasingly at a distance after CAN'T BUY ME LOVE, the first Beatles single to feature only one singer.

With its bobbing beat and light acoustic rhythm, CAN'T BUY ME LOVE prefaced the second phase of The Beatles career: that of global recognition and 'standard' status. Its effortless rightness – from McCartney's boisterous vocal (beginning three beats before the rest join in) to Harrison's first wholly memorable guitar solo – bespeaks a band of talents on top of their world. Their teenage ambition to displace Elvis Presley from the ruling summit of pop is achieved here.

6 A Hard Day's Night
(Lennon–McCartney)

Lennon double-tracked vocal, electric and acoustic
rhythm guitars; **McCartney** double-tracked vocal, bass;
Harrison lead guitar; **Starr** drums, bongos; **George
Martin** piano.
Recorded: 16 April 1964, Abbey Road 2.
Producer: George Martin. Engineer: Norman Smith.
UK release: 10 July 1964 (A single/THINGS WE SAID
TODAY).
US release: 26 June 1964 (LP: *A Hard Day's Night*).

The mighty opening chord of A HARD DAY'S NIGHT (G
eleventh suspended fourth) has a significance in Beatles
lore matched only by the concluding E major of A DAY
IN THE LIFE, the two opening and closing the group's
middle period of peak creativity. Their rivals must have
heard this portentous sound with awe. Apart from Bob
Dylan, none could match such an impression of
panoramic sweep and power.

Seven weeks of shooting for *A Hard Day's Night* intervened between this and the group's previous session, and they went straight back to location work in London after it. The title had been uttered by Starr after an exhausting day's filming on 19 March. Bandied about as a priceless witticism during the next three weeks, it was officially adopted for the film in mid-April, at which point Lennon hurried home to ensure that it was he and not McCartney who wrote the song. ([5] CAN'T BUY ME LOVE, with which McCartney had stolen a march on him, was then at No. 1 on both sides of the Atlantic.) A typically horizontal modal melody, it was soon finished, whereupon Lennon convened the group and it was recorded the following day – the shortest interval between writing and recording of any Beatles song not made up in the studio.

Taped in mono, the backing track was achieved on the fifth of nine takes. Following this, Lennon and McCartney did their vocals, tracking them before adding bongos, extra percussion and another acoustic guitar. Harrison's solo, doubled on piano by Martin, was taped at half-speed, as was the jangling arpeggiated fade. The latter, so influential on The Byrds, consists of a tick-tocking swing between a fifthless Am7 and F major, each contained within the song's opening chord (neither major nor minor). Acting coincidentally as a musical pointer to the major/minor structures used throughout the album, it was part of the concept from the first take, presumably envisaged by Lennon as a transition from the film's main titles to the first scene. With this powerful, bluesy song – a performance made incandescent by Starr's excited contribution – The Beatles completed the seven titles required for the soundtrack.

7 **Eight Days A Week**
(Lennon–McCartney)

Lennon vocal, acoustic rhythm guitar, handclaps;
McCartney vocal, bass, handclaps; **Harrison** vocal, lead
guitar, handclaps; **Starr** drums, handclaps.
Recorded: 6, 18 October 1964, Abbey Road 2.
Producer: George Martin. Engineer: Norman Smith.
UK release: 4 December 1964 (LP: *Beatles For Sale)*.
US release: 15 February 1965 (A single/I DON'T WANT
TO SPOIL THE PARTY).

Supposedly written as a title-track for The Beatles'
second film, scheduled to start shooting five months
later, EIGHT DAYS A WEEK was brought into the studio
by McCartney in an unfinished state. As with [6] A HARD
DAY'S NIGHT, the title derived from a standard
Liverpudlianism attributed to Starr. Lennon joined his
partner in writing a middle eight and together they
worked out a harmonised introduction which they toyed
with in several ways before dropping it on take 6. The

track was finished in seven more takes, during which
the melody of the title-phrase was changed. Edit-sections
for the intro and ending were added during the album's
penultimate session twelve days later.

With a classic McCartney walking bass, EIGHT DAYS
A WEEK swaggers up and down the scale of D major
much like ALL MY LOVING in E. Again like ALL MY
LOVING, it shows signs of having been worked out on a
piano (particularly the four-bar bridge – 'Hold me, love
me' – with its harmony in perfect fourths and concluding
diminished G sharp). Nothing in the throwaway lyric
would have been out of place in the group's 1963 output
and the brilliant simplicity of the whole thing has 'hit
single' written all over it. Unfortunately for McCartney,
Lennon was about to produce [8] I FEEL FINE – the riff
from which he insisted on doodling between takes – and
its author had to wait until March 1965 to see EIGHT
DAYS A WEEK lodge for two weeks at No. 1 in America,
where it was issued after I FEEL FINE had held the same
position for three weeks in January.

Lennon later thought little of this song, implying that
it was superficial – yet no such attitude can be detected
in his vocal, which is sung with the excitement of the
creative moment. (Why McCartney didn't sing lead is

unknown. Possibly the key suited Lennon better; or perhaps the brassy glare of his double-tracked voice was recognised by McCartney as more effective.) On any list of pop records that capture the soaring sunshine optimism of the mid-Sixties, EIGHT DAYS A WEEK would be near the top, along with [4] I WANT TO HOLD YOUR HAND and [17] PENNY LANE. Musically less involving than either of them, it holds its place with its sheer verve and the embracing warmth of its sound, whose texture of carillon electric lead and chiming acoustics was so influential on the nascent American folk-rock scene.

8 I Feel Fine (*Lennon–McCartney*)

Lennon double-tracked vocal, lead/rhythm guitar;
McCartney harmony vocal, bass; **Harrison** harmony
vocal, lead/rhythm guitar; **Starr** drums.
Recorded: 18 October 1964, Abbey Road 2.
Producer: George Martin. Engineer: Norman Smith.
UK release: 27 November 1964 (A single/SHE'S A
WOMAN).
US release: 23 November 1964 (A single/SHE'S A
WOMAN).

Following KANSAS CITY and the remake of MR
MOONLIGHT, the group turned to Lennon's new song I
FEEL FINE, written – or at any rate begun – 'at a recording
session' and now intended as the next single. ([7] EIGHT
DAYS A WEEK had been first choice as recently as six
days earlier, with I'M A LOSER and NO REPLY as other
contenders.) Lennon's competitive need to get the A-side
here produced an unusually straightforward expression
of well-being, couched, like McCartney's eagerly

commercial EIGHT DAYS A WEEK, in the artless terms of their early lyrics. Like SHE'S A WOMAN, I FEEL FINE is a mutated blues (making this pairing the second Beatles single to be based on blues changes) but there's nothing depressive about the song, which takes its effervescent mood, as well as its form, from the difficult guitar riff which Lennon and Harrison play, often in unison, more or less throughout.

The track opens with a sustained low A on bass as a foundation for feedback from Lennon's Rickenbacker (obtained by striking the note with the volume switch down and then turning up while pointing the pickups towards his amp). He was inordinately proud of this in later years – 'The first time feedback was used on record' – and the effect is often cited as The Beatles' first recording experiment. However, McCartney can claim precedence in three cases, all (like I FEEL FINE) recorded in the first flush of the group's encounter with marijuana: the overdriven guitar and drop-in piano of WHAT YOU'RE DOING, the pioneering fade-in to EIGHT DAYS A WEEK, and the generally *outré* SHE'S A WOMAN. As for the origin of Lennon's feedback inspiration, he later conceded that 'everyone' then playing live was using it. For electric guitarists, feedback is a hazard of amplification, to be either avoided or incorporated into their sound in a controlled way. The only local guitarist using feedback as pure noise in 1964 was Pete Townshend, soon to manipulate the effect spectacularly in The Who's outrageous second single 'Anyway Anyhow Anywhere'. A couple of days after recording I'M A LOSER, The Beatles shared a Blackpool bill with The High Numbers (a few weeks before they became The Who). Did Lennon – as he had after hearing harmonica-player Delbert McClinton at the Tower Ballroom, New Brighton, two years earlier – mark, learn and inwardly digest?

Recorded in nine takes, I FEEL FINE, far from a brand new number, sounds like something the group had been playing for years. The lack of a conventional rhythm guitar opens the sound out, allowing the syncopations in the riff to spark and jump. Responding to this, Starr turns in a buoyant performance, playing Latin-style on the ride-cymbal with conga accents on the high tom-tom. Considering that it's mostly his energy that lifts the track – for instance, coming out of the middle eights (0:54, 1:50) – it's unfortunate that the production parks him far left in the stereo spectrum rather than in the middle. Harrison's four-bar guitar break similarly distils the overall feel of the track: not so much a solo as a pithy summary of its bluesy mood and form. Though not an outstanding song, I FEEL FINE went straight to No. 1 in the UK where it resided for six weeks. In America, its stay at the top was shorter, though its B-side, SHE'S A WOMAN, climbed to No. 4 on the strength of point-of-sale requests.

9 Ticket To Ride *(Lennon–McCartney)*

Lennon double-tracked vocal, rhythm guitar; **McCartney** harmony vocal, bass, lead guitar; **Harrison** harmony vocal, rhythm guitar; **Starr** drums, tambourine, handclaps.
Recorded: 15 February 1965, Abbey Road 2.
Producer: George Martin. Engineer: Norman Smith.
UK release: 9 April 1965 (A single/YES IT IS).
US release: 19 April 1965 (A single/YES IT IS).

Following their UK tour at the end of 1964 and another long Christmas season, the group took a month off before starting work on the second of their films. At this stage entitled *Eight Arms To Hold You*, the project was ill-conceived, swiftly degenerating into a whimsical working holiday in the Bahamas and Austria. In the week before they flew to Nassau, The Beatles met at Abbey Road to start work on the soundtrack album, returning to Studio 2 on the day that [7] EIGHT DAYS A WEEK arrived at No. 1 in America. They began with their new single, a Lennon number.

A bitter, dissonant mid-tempo song with a dragging beat, TICKET TO RIDE was hardly an obvious choice for a Beatles single and there was said to be disagreement about it behind the scenes. In the run-up to its UK issue, the pop press trailed it as a new departure for the group: something unusual, even uncommercial. In the event, while British record buyers kept it at No. 1 for three weeks, America was less impressed, purchasing enough copies to haul it laboriously to the top for one week before it was deposed by The Beach Boys' cheery 'Help Me Rhonda'. With its melancholy B-side YES IT IS, TICKET TO RIDE was psychologically deeper than anything The Beatles had recorded before and a sharp anomaly in a pop scene where doomy melodramas from balladeers like Gene Pitney and P. J. Proby stood in for real feeling.

Yet there was more to the record than unusual emotional depth. As sheer sound, TICKET TO RIDE is extraordinary for its time – massive with chiming electric guitars, weighty rhythm and rumbling floor tom-toms. Among the first attempts to convey on record the impact achievable live by an amplified group, it was later recalled by Lennon as 'one of the earliest heavy metal records'. As such, he may have been going for the effect he'd heard The Who produce seven months earlier, though it must be said that interest in the possibilities of amplified sound was very much in the air around this time. Apart from The Who's as-yet unrecorded ventures in pure noise, Jeff Beck, a master of controlled feedback, was about to replace bluesman Eric Clapton as lead guitarist with one of Britain's most exciting live groups, The Yardbirds. A tougher sound had also entered the UK singles chart towards the end of 1964 with The Animals' 'I'm Crying', The Kinks' 'You Really Got Me', Them's 'Baby Please Don't Go', and Keith Richards' ferocious minimalist solo in The Rolling Stones' 'It's All Over Now'. Having played acoustic guitar throughout most of *A Hard Day's Night* and *Beatles For Sale*, Lennon returned to electric guitar in [8] I FEEL FINE and TICKET TO RIDE with an energy drawn partly from the air of adventure then abroad on the UK scene. But there was perhaps a more potent reason for his renewed absorption in the texture of high amplification.

Some time early in 1965 – the exact date is unknown but it may have been in January or February, before The Beatles went abroad to film *Help!* – Lennon and Harrison encountered LSD. 'Spiked' by a foolish acquaintance who slipped it into their coffee after dinner, they found themselves careering through late-night London,

dazzled and near-hysterical as the powerful hallu-
cinogen took effect. Lennon later admitted that the experience had stunned him, revealing a mode of perception
which marijuana had barely hinted at. Whether TICKET
TO RIDE was his first creative response to LSD is, on
current evidence, impossible to say. Its heavy rhythm
and immersion in electric sound may have been a spin-
off from the cannabis inspiration audible in the later
work for *Beatles For Sale*. On the other hand, the track
is far more intense than anything The Beatles made in
late 1964, pointing forward to 1966 and such frankly
psychedelic records as RAIN, which shares its gong-like
clangour of saturated guitar tone, and TOMORROW NEVER
KNOWS, which emulates its high-lying one-note bass-line
and broken drum pattern. (It also shows signs of 1966-
style varispeeding, being pitched in the gap between G
sharp and A.) TICKET TO RIDE is even more unusual for
The Beatles in clinging, entranced, to its opening chord
for six long bars (ten, including the introduction). Like
the middle eight experiments on *Beatles For Sale*, this
was clearly deliberate and may, in this case, have been
suggested by Martha and the Vandellas' similarly obses-
sional 'one-chord' hits for Motown towards the end of
1964: 'Dancing in the Street' and 'Wild One'. Again

anticipating 1966, Lennon's melody rises and falls in mesmeric *raga*-style – A, C sharp, D, E, G – making McCartney's harmony in bluesy fourths and thirds seem shockingly harsh.

Though it had appeared in half a dozen Beatle songs, the word 'sad' here carries a weight graphically embodied in the track's oppressive pedal tonality and deliberately cumbersome drums. There is, too, a narcotic passivity about Lennon's lyric: though the girl is leaving him, he makes no attempt to stop or threaten her as he would have done in earlier songs; all he does – in the ruminative, monochordal middle eight – is mutter bitterly while she 'rides high', absorbed in herself (a self whose chief characteristic is that of not caring). By 1966, according to Lennon, he was 'eating' LSD, taking 'thousands' of trips and lapsing into introspective states for days on end. This self-centred, addictive outlook, which eventually led him to heroin, is vividly prefigured in the droning sound and lethargic mood of TICKET TO RIDE. The first Beatles recording to break the three-minute barrier, it is an extraordinary precognition of their next stage of development, commenced fifteen months later with TOMORROW NEVER KNOWS.

10 **Help!** *(Lennon–McCartney)*

Lennon double-tracked vocal, acoustic rhythm guitar;
McCartney backing vocal, bass; **Harrison** backing vocal,
lead guitar; **Starr** drums, tambourine.
Recorded: 13 April 1965, Abbey Road 2.
Producer: George Martin. Engineer: Norman Smith.
UK release: 23 July 1965 (A single/I'M DOWN).
US release: 19 July 1965 (A single/I'M DOWN).

Seven weeks into shooting, The Beatles' second film was
still scheduled as *Eight Arms To Hold You*, yet neither
Lennon nor McCartney fancied writing a song to accommodate this octopodous concept, and in the end director
Richard Lester, perhaps acknowledging the slapdash
and directionless tone of the project, decided on *Help!*.
Written almost entirely by Lennon at his new home in
Weybridge, the title song began in mid-tempo, but was
speeded up slightly during recording to make it more
commercial. Lennon later resented this for compro-
mising his conception, yet the group needed another hit

and the job they did in sprucing up his first thoughts was comparable to the similarly effective work on PLEASE PLEASE ME and [3] SHE LOVES YOU.

In fact, HELP! retains its authenticity through the emotion in its author's voice. Looking back on this song in 1980, Lennon recalled it as a cry for help from the depths of what he referred to as his 'fat Elvis' period. Mentally exhausted by two years of continuous touring, he was isolated and alienated in his multi-roomed mansion in the stockbroker belt of London's western fringe. His marriage damaged by his orgiastic round of whores and groupies on the road, he felt unsustained by his faithful and attentive wife Cynthia, who, concerned for her husband's health, made no secret of disapproving of his drug intake. All of this amounted to a personal malaise that would expand to overwhelming dimensions during the next two years.

Lyrically, HELP! distils Lennon's misery, marking a watershed in his life. Here, the shell he had grown around his feelings since his mother's death finally cracks as he admits a need for others. Musically, the song offers neither artifice nor distance. So characteristically horizontal that its verse consists of one repeated note trailing off into a wail, the song opens on an unhappy B minor, climbing stepwise via a sixth to a pleading scream as A major arrives to stabilise the harmony. (This sequence is a condensation of the chorus.) With no relieving middle eight – its role usurped by a repeat of the first verse – HELP! perpetually slides back to the anxiety and tension of B minor. Only in the song's moaning final sixth is this tension wearily resolved.

Despite a recording gap of nearly two months, The Beatles picked up where they'd left off with YOU'RE GOING TO LOSE THAT GIRL, developing a similarly complex backing-vocal pattern, this time anticipating rather than responding to the melody. This arrangement, plus a duplicate of Lennon's lead vocal, were added on takes 9 and 10. To finish, Starr overdubbed tambourine and Harrison taped his guitar part, descending at the end of each chorus on a cross-rhythm arpeggio run in the style of Nashville guitarist Chet Atkins. (This, and Starr's straight-quaver fills against the song's fast shuffle beat, are good examples of the group's care in painting characterful touches into every corner of their best work.)

Taken into The Beatles' act during 1965, HELP! rose to No. 1 on both sides of the Atlantic. In America it displaced Sonny and Cher's 'I Got You Babe' and was succeeded by Barry McGuire's nuclear-protest song 'Eve of Destruction', representatives of a new style pioneered by Dylan and his acolytes The Byrds: folk-rock. Sold as America's answer to the 'British Invasion' of groups from Liverpool and London in 1964, the folk-rock phenomenon coincided with the US Labor Department's panicky protectionist move to ban British acts from America. Beatles-business, though, was too lucrative to exclude and they accordingly returned to the States in August 1965 to promote HELP! and the thinly inconsequential film to which it was formally attached (and which they loathed).

11 **Yesterday** *(Lennon–McCartney)*

McCartney vocal, acoustic guitar; **Tony Gilbert, Sidney Sax** violins; **Kenneth Essex** viola; **Francisco Gabarro** cello.
Recorded: 14, 17 June 1965, Abbey Road 2.
Producer: George Martin. Engineer: Norman Smith.
UK release: 6 August 1965 (LP: *Help!*).
US release: 13 September 1966 (A single/ACT NATURALLY).

According to George Martin, McCartney wrote YESTERDAY while staying at the George V hotel, Paris, in January 1964 (i.e., during the writing stage for the *A Hard Day's Night* album). If true, it would mean that this famous piece, which holds the *Guinness Book of Records* title as the most 'covered' song in history, was left off two Beatles albums and withheld until the final stages of a third before being considered good enough to record – on the face of it, not very likely. It is, however, true that McCartney was hesitant about YESTERDAY for several months, playing it to friends and asking them, 'Is this by someone else or did I write it?', unable to believe that it hadn't been around for at least a generation.

His uncertainty stemmed from the circumstances of its composition. Waking one day with the tune running through his head, he stumbled to a piano to work out the chords. In effect, YESTERDAY fell, fully-formed, out of the sky. 'When you're trying to write a song,' he later observed, 'there are certain times when you get the essence, it's all there. It's like an egg being laid – not a crack or flaw in it.' While not the only Beatles song to arrive in this quasi-mediumistic way, YESTERDAY remains the uncanniest instance of it in the group's discography. (Not that the legend of its flawlessness is justified, its middle eight being perceptibly less inspired than its verse/chorus.)

McCartney sang YESTERDAY accompanied by his Epiphone Texan guitar on the evening of 14 June, only two hours after he had rounded off the afternoon with the shrieking choruses of I'M DOWN. (Though no modern producer would dream of allowing a singer to risk his larynx on a screamer before taping a delicate ballad, this, insists McCartney, is how he was happy to do it.) A score for string quartet – George Martin's first major arranging contribution to The Beatles' discography – was over-dubbed three days later on the afternoon of 17 June, before the recording of ACT NATURALLY. McCartney was sceptical about strings and stipulated that he didn't want it to end up 'like Mantovani'. Even after Martin had played him some quartet records, he remained adamant that there should be no *vibrato*. Aware that modern string-players would find this unnatural, Martin diverted McCartney by asking him to supervise the arrangement, as a result of which the latter added the cello phrase in bar 4 of the middle eight (1:25–1:27) and the violin's held high A in the final verse. The result has an austere clarity which, despite minor imperfections, deserves the praise showered on it. Issued as a single in the USA, it defied American popular distaste for the 'highbrow' by staying at No. 1 for a month.

With its yearning suspended ninths, rapid harmonic movement and irregular phrase-lengths, YESTERDAY has been analysed more closely than any other Beatles composition. Its significance, so far as the group was concerned, lay less in the song's musical attributes than in George Martin's disclosure to them of an hitherto unsuspected world of classical instrumental colour. Restrained by the demands of touring, they paused a year before putting this discovery to full use.

12 **Day Tripper** *(Lennon–McCartney)*

Lennon double-tracked vocal, rhythm/lead guitar;
McCartney double-tracked vocal, bass; **Harrison** lead
guitar; **Starr** drums, tambourine.
Recorded: 16 October 1965, Abbey Road 2.
Producer: George Martin. Engineer: Norman Smith.
UK release: 3 December 1965 (A single/WE CAN WORK
IT OUT).
US release: 6 December 1965 (A single/WE CAN WORK IT
OUT).

Returning to the studio on Saturday after a day off, The
Beatles maintained the bluesy style of DRIVE MY CAR
with a song Lennon and McCartney later admitted had
been 'forced' by the need for a new single. Conceivably
they wrote DAY TRIPPER on Friday after consulting a
rough mix of DRIVE MY CAR, which would explain why
Thursday's session overran. Entirely dependent on its
riff – catchier if far less subtle than the line used on
DRIVE MY CAR – DAY TRIPPER repaid what its companion

track had stolen from Otis Redding. (Tickled by what he heard, Redding cut his own, madly up-tempo, version of DAY TRIPPER for Stax in 1967.)

Though Lennon had yet to launch himself into his full-scale LSD period, he evidently felt sufficiently versed in the 'counterculture' associated with the drug to poke fun at those who took it without changing their outlook. The lyric of DAY TRIPPER, he later explained, was an attack on 'weekend hippies' – those who donned floral shirts and headbands to listen to 'acid rock' between 9-to-5 office jobs. While something of the sort may have been in Lennon's mind in October 1965, it must be said that few outside a select circle in America had taken LSD by then, that the word 'hippie' was not coined until 1966, and that 'acid rock' arrived a full year later. The lyric may, in fact, be partly about McCartney's reluctance to experiment with the drug and partly to do with the aloof heroine of NORWEGIAN WOOD. (The line recorded as 'she's a big teaser' was originally written as 'she's a prick teaser'.) Either way it isn't very interesting, despite sustaining the strain of ironic narrative introduced in the group's previous two recordings.

Recorded with peculiarly wide stereo separation, DAY TRIPPER starts as a twelve-bar in E which makes a feint at turning into a twelve-bar in the relative minor (i.e., the chorus) before doubling back to the expected B – another joke from a group which had clearly decided that wit was to be their new gimmick. Reaching B by this erratic route the second time round, the song hangs onto it in a twelve-bar pedal-point crescendo over which Lennon solos while Harrison climbs a lengthy scale ending triumphantly in the home key. (Another in-joke occurs in the chorus bars of Starr's drum-part, played with fours on the bass-drum in the style of Al Jackson of The MGs, the Stax house band.) Musically uninspired by The Beatles' standards and marred by a bad punch-in edit on the vocal track (1:50), DAY TRIPPER was nevertheless scheduled as their new single until the recording of [13] WE CAN WORK IT OUT a few days later. Arguments over which was to be given preference (Lennon wanted DAY TRIPPER) led to the single being marketed as the first 'double A-side'. Airplay and point-of-sale requests soon proved WE CAN WORK IT OUT to be more popular.

13 **We Can Work It Out**
(Lennon–McCartney)

McCartney double-tracked vocal, bass; **Lennon** harmony
vocal, acoustic rhythm guitar, harmonium; **Harrison**
harmony vocal (?); **Starr** drums, tambourine.
Recorded: 20, 29 October 1965, Abbey Road 2.
Producer: George Martin. Engineer: Norman Smith.
UK release: 3 December 1965 (A single/DAY TRIPPER).
US release: 6 December 1965 (A single/DAY TRIPPER).

The result of by far the largest amount of studio time
devoted to a Beatles track thus far (eleven hours), WE
CAN WORK IT OUT is a classic instance of Lennon and
McCartney collaborating as equals. McCartney wrote
the words and music to the eight-bar verse/chorus,
Lennon the words and music to the sixteen-bar middle.
Based on McCartney's often fractious relationship with
Jane Asher, the song unburdens itself with vivid urgency.
The usual critical line, derived from Lennon's remark
to this effect to *Playboy* in 1980, is that his section is

impatiently realistic beside the cajoling optimism of McCartney's part. This, though, misreads the song, which is not only tersely forthright throughout, but tough in passages which Lennon had no hand in. Something of a breakthrough for McCartney, his part of the lyric for WE CAN WORK IT OUT displays a dramatic instinct which would soon begin to dominate his work.

Melodically, McCartney's D major verse is unusually full of repetitions, implying that it was written under the pressure of emotional necessity rather than out of purely formal inspiration. With its tense suspensions and irregular phrase-lengths, it shows him at his most Lennonish, directly expressing the forcefulness of his lyric. Lennon's middle eight – one of his cleverest – shifts focus from McCartney's concrete reality to a philosophical perspective in B minor, illustrating this with a churchy suspension and a burlesque waltz that prefigures the solemn dance of Henry the Horse in BEING FOR THE BENEFIT OF MR KITE! This was probably meant to suggest tiresome struggle, but doubles as an ironic image of the *karmic* roundabout of heedless egoism, a concept with which Lennon would have been familiar from exchanges with Harrison. These passages are so suited to his Salvation Army harmonium that it's hard to imagine them not being composed on it. The swell-pedal crescendos he adds to the verses are, on the other hand, textural washes added in the studio – the first of their kind on a Beatles record and signposts to the enriched sound-palette of *Revolver*.

Produced with restraint despite the twelve hours spent on it, WE CAN WORK IT OUT was an understandable favourite of its authors, who met more closely in a single song only in their masterpiece A DAY IN THE LIFE. It was an inevitable No. 1 on both sides of the Atlantic, becoming The Beatles' fastest-selling single since CAN'T BUY ME LOVE, their previous McCartney-led A-side in Britain. Despite his last-ditch attempt at promoting [12] DAY TRIPPER to the A-side, Lennon must have sensed that his era of dominance over the band's output, begun with YOU CAN'T DO THAT, was over. From now on, his partner would be in the ascendant not only as a songwriter, but also as instrumentalist, arranger, producer and *de facto* musical director of The Beatles.

14 **Paperback Writer**
(Lennon–McCartney)

McCartney vocal, bass; **Lennon** backing vocal, rhythm guitar; **Harrison** backing vocal, lead guitar; **Starr** drums, tambourine.

Recorded: 13, 14 April 1966, Abbey Road 3.
Producer: George Martin. Engineer: Geoff Emerick.
UK release: 10 June 1966 (A single/RAIN).
US release: 30 May 1966 (A single/RAIN).

The Beatles' twelfth British single was their first since [3] SHE LOVES YOU not to go straight to No. 1 in the UK. Written by McCartney – the second of a run of three consecutive A-sides by him – it strained too hard to define a new style for the group, its air of contrivance sounding flashy after the ideal balance of form and feeling in [13] WE CAN WORK IT OUT. Displaying The Beatles' cannabis-induced fascination with getting the maximum out of one chord, PAPERBACK WRITER offers a jokey lyric reflecting its era of classless ambition: the generation of 'young meteors' who in the mid-Sixties rose from provincial and working-class backgrounds to dazzle the heights of British fashion, film and print. Beyond this social observation any potential poignancy is sacrificed to excitement, word games and studio effects. In the end, this is a record less about its time and place than about pop records in early 1966. Intermittently glimpsed in The Beatles' music, 'Swinging London' was less interesting to them as visiting north-erners than it was to cynical locals like The Kinks and The Rolling Stones.

Now living within walking distance of Abbey Road (in Cavendish Avenue, St John's Wood), McCartney was often at the studio before the others, trying out musical ideas and production effects which he then presented to them as *faits accomplis*. While the group benefited immensely from his energetic attention to detail, it didn't make him popular and his pedantic insistence on Harrison playing every guitar line *just* so often caused tension. (Whether he or Harrison recorded the guitar riff on PAPERBACK WRITER is unknown, though it's clearly McCartney's idea – based, as Lennon later remarked, on the similar figure in [12] DAY TRIPPER.)

Made in eleven hours, the track has a widely divided

stereo image using, among other novelties, a drum part channelled separately across the spectrum (snare and cymbals left, tom-toms centre, bass-drum right). For his prominent high-register bass part, McCartney swapped his Hofner for the long-scale Rickenbacker, a guitar with a solid, cutting treble tone which he modified by miking his amp through a second speaker and rolling off the top with compression to get a smoother sound. With a tape-echoed chorus, the vocal arrangement includes passages of four-part polyphony modelled on The Beach Boys, whose 'Sloop John B' had just entered the UK charts. That Lennon and Harrison were not entirely serious in performing their falsetto parts can be heard in the gasps of laughter audible on a very 'dirty' vocal track (and the fact that, during the second verse/chorus, they are chanting 'Frère Jacques').

15 **Eleanor Rigby** (*Lennon–McCartney*)

McCartney vocal; **Lennon** harmony vocal; **Harrison** harmony vocal; **Tony Gilbert, Sidney Sax, John Sharpe, Jurgen Hess** violins; **Stephen Shingles, John Underwood** violas; **Derek Simpson, Norman Jones** cellos.

Recorded: 28 April 1966, Abbey Road 2; 2 April, 6 June 1966, Abbey Road 3.

Producer: George Martin. Engineer: Geoff Emerick.

UK release: 5 August 1966 (LP: *Revolver*).

US release: 8 August 1966 (LP: *Revolver*).

Death is a subject normally avoided in pop music. Where acknowledged, it is either sanitised with heavenly choirs or treated as a black joke (e.g., The Shangri-Las' camp 1965 classic 'Leader of the Pack'). Consequently, the downbeat demise of a lonely spinster in ELEANOR RIGBY – not to mention the brutal image of the priest 'wiping the dirt from his hands as he walks from the grave' – came as quite a shock to pop listeners in 1966. Taken together with George Martin's wintry string octet arrangement, the impact was transfixing.

In fact, the song's grim final verse was settled on only after much head-scratching and at the last minute. According to McCartney, ELEANOR RIGBY began as a plain tune with a melancholy descending phrase and the image of a spinster, Miss Daisy Hawkins, sweeping up the rice in a church after a marriage. Meeting Jane Asher in Bristol, where she was working in rep, McCartney allegedly got the name Rigby from a clothes shop, adding 'Eleanor' from Eleanor Bron, the actress who had played the female lead in *Help!*. Against this is the fact that the Rigbys were a well-known local family in Liverpool, of whom one, Eleanor (1895–1939), lies buried in the churchyard of St Peter's in Woolton, close to McCartney's home suburb of Allerton.

Armed with only the first verse, McCartney headed for Lennon's house at Weybridge where, during an informal evening with friends, he and the other Beatles pieced the rest of the song together. Starting as Father McCartney, the priest in the second verse soon became the more neutral Father MacKenzie, a name found by consulting a telephone directory. Starr suggested the idea of him 'darning his socks in the night'. The refrain 'Ah look at all the lonely people' seems to have been designed by committee, possibly later in the studio (where some say the last verse was decided); others maintain that the song was completed during the same evening. (Lennon, who subsequently claimed 'about 70 per cent' of the lyric, apparently tried to quash the idea of its two characters 'meeting' at the end.)

Given its chaotic genesis, ELEANOR RIGBY is extraordinarily cogent and concentrated. The face that the heroine 'keeps in a jar by the door' (to mask the despair inadmissible by English middle-class etiquette) remains the single most memorable image in The Beatles' output. Yet the lyric's televisual vividness ('Look at him working') is never gratuitous, being consistently at the service of the song's relentless despondency. Eleanor Rigby dies alone because she is unable to tell anyone how she felt. MacKenzie's sermon won't be heard – not that he cares very much about his parishioners – because religious faith has perished along with communal spirit ('No one was saved'). Often represented as purveyors of escapist fantasy, The Beatles were, at their best, more poignantly realistic about their society than any other popular artists of their time.

The monochrome pessimism of the lyric is paralleled in the naked simplicity of the music: a plain E Dorian melody over what amounts to two chords. Arranged by Martin from a rough idea by McCartney, the string accompaniment was recorded along with a guide vocal in a standard three-hour session, the final vocals being added later. Issued as a single (coupled with [16] YELLOW SUBMARINE), ELEANOR RIGBY held the UK No. 1 spot for four weeks during August and September. (The comparatively hollow [14] PAPERBACK WRITER lasted only two weeks at the top.) In militantly optimistic America, however, the combination fared less well, YELLOW SUBMARINE's light relief proving more popular. Neither reached the top of the chart.

16 Yellow Submarine
(Lennon–McCartney)

Starr vocal, drums; **McCartney** backing vocal, shouting, bass; **Lennon** backing vocal, shouting, acoustic guitar; **Harrison** backing vocal, tambourine; **Mal Evans** bass drum; **Mal Evans, Neil Aspinall, George Martin, Geoff Emerick, Patti Harrison, Brian Jones, Marianne Faithfull, Alf Bicknell** backing vocals.

Recorded: 26 May 1966, Abbey Road 3; 1 June 1966, Abbey Road 2.

Producer: George Martin. Engineer: Geoff Emerick.

UK release: 5 August 1966 (LP: *Revolver*).

US release: 8 August 1966 (LP: *Revolver*).

Written in bed one night as a children's song, McCartney's YELLOW SUBMARINE may have been a musical spin-off from Bob Dylan's march-tempo 'Rainy Day Women Nos 12 and 35', which entered the UK chart a fortnight before. The Beatles met Dylan at the Savoy Hotel the evening before they began the track, where they also ran into Donovan, with whom they got on well. The following day McCartney stopped off at Donovan's apartment and played him YELLOW SUBMARINE, asking for a suggestion for the closing lines. The latter obliged with 'Sky of blue, sea of green'. That evening, after much rehearsal, the group taped a rhythm track with vocals, returning a week later to throw a party in Studio 2 and dub on sound effects. Directed by George Martin, whose experience as a producer of comedy records now came into its own, they raided Abbey Road's 'trap room' for its trove of noise-making implements, including chains, whistles, hooters, hoses, handbells and an old tin bath. In his element, Lennon filled a bucket with water and blew bubbles in it while the group's chauffeur Alf Bicknell rattled chains in the bath and Brian Jones of The Rolling Stones clinked glasses. Other effects were obtained from records, including an uncredited 78rpm snippet of a brass band march cut up by Martin and cleverly pasted into the last two bars of the second verse. For the central section, Lennon and McCartney went into the studio's echo chamber to yell meaningless nauticalisms, Lennon remaining there to repeat Starr's lines, Goon-style, throughout the final verse.

All told, this process took nearly twelve hours – time well-spent in producing a sparkling novelty song impossible to dislike.

17 **Penny Lane** *(Lennon–McCartney)*

McCartney vocal, pianos, bass, harmonium, tambourine, effects; **Lennon** backing vocal, pianos, guitar, congas, hand-claps; **Harrison** backing vocal, guitar; **Starr** drums, hand-bell; **George Martin** piano; **Ray Swinfield, P. Goody, Manny Winters, Dennis Walton** flutes, piccolos; **David Mason, Leon Calvert, Freddy Clayton, Bert Courtley, Duncan Campbell** trumpets, flugelhorn; **Dick Morgan, Mike Winfield** oboes, cor anglais; **Frank Clarke** double bass.

Recorded: 29, 30 December 1966, 4, 6, 9 January 1967, Abbey Road 2; 10, 12 January 1967, Abbey Road 3; 17 January 1967, Abbey Road 2.

Producer: George Martin. Engineer: Geoff Emerick.

UK release: 17 February 1967 (A single/STRAWBERRY FIELDS FOREVER).

US release: 13 February 1967 (A single/STRAWBERRY FIELDS FOREVER).

Anyone unlucky enough not to have been aged between

fourteen and thirty during 1966–7 will never know the excitement of those years in popular culture. A sunny optimism permeated everything and possibilities seemed limitless. Bestriding a British scene that embraced music, poetry, fashion and film, and in which English football had recently beaten the world, The Beatles were at their peak and looked up to in awe as arbiters of a positive new age in which the dead customs of the older generation would be refreshed and remade through the creative energy of the classless young. With its vision of 'blue suburban skies' and boundlessly confident vigour, PENNY LANE distils the spirit of that time more perfectly than any other creative product of the mid-Sixties. Couched in the primary colours of a picture-book, yet observed with the slyness of a gang of kids straggling home from school, PENNY LANE is both naive and knowing – but above all thrilled to be alive.

Lennon and McCartney had toyed with this title for eighteen months, having made a list of Liverpool place-names during a writing session for *Rubber Soul*. While it was Lennon who picked the neighbourhood in question, it was McCartney who went on to set it to music. Both, though, contributed to the pictorial lyric which was very specific to the actual place. As Lennon later told

Rolling Stone: 'The bank was *there*, and *that* was where the tram sheds were and people waiting and the inspector stood *there*, the fire engines were down *there*. It was just reliving childhood.'

The track's distinctive staccato piano chords (to become a cliché in the hands of imitators) recycle the style first tried in GOT TO GET YOU INTO MY LIFE. So successful was the effect in PENNY LANE that McCartney quickly repeated it in different tempi in four more songs: FIXING A HOLE, GETTING BETTER, WITH A LITTLE HELP FROM MY FRIENDS and YOUR MOTHER SHOULD KNOW. If, in PENNY LANE, this device seems simple, the actual sound of it was the product of hard work, guided by its author's interest in production effects. Presumably playing to a click-track, he began with a basic take of piano chords. Having added a second piano (sent, with reverb, through a Vox amp), he recorded a third at half-speed, thereby altering the instrument's overtones. On top of this three-decked super-piano were layered various 'treated' percussion effects and some high-frequency tones from a harmonium. Bounced down to accommodate a guide-vocal (taped, for some reason, at reduced speed), the track was left to mature over Christmas. Work on it resumed early in January 1967 with a fourth piano layer overdubbed by Lennon and, two days later, yet more piano from Lennon and Martin. At this point McCartney finally approved the sound. Further slowed recording was applied to his bass guitar and most of the rest of the group's other overdubs; however, the famous B-flat piccolo trumpet solo added on the final day of recording was, contrary to legend, taped in real time and not speeded up. (Or so says David Mason, the Philharmonia trumpeter who performed the part. Few would doubt his claim that he can, to this day, play the line along with the record, but this is no proof that the track wasn't varispeeded – without his knowledge – during the recording.)

Following the style created in *Revolver*, PENNY LANE is packed with illustrative sound effects and arrangement touches, ranging from the obvious (the fireman's handbell) to the virtually inaudible (an arthritic double bass depicting the Banker lowering himself into the Barber's chair for a trim). While a team effort in terms of performance, the track is as essentially McCartneyesque as STRAWBERRY FIELDS FOREVER is Lennonian. Breezily vertical in tune and harmony where STRAWBERRY FIELDS is lazily horizontal, PENNY LANE's jaunty triplet melody, counterpointed by a high-lying bass, could have come from no other songwriter. Credit must also be given to him for David Mason's quasi-baroque trumpet solo. Though Martin wrote it out, the line, like other details of the arrangement, was sung to him by McCartney in imitation of Bach's Second Brandenburg Concerto, which he had heard on television, played by Mason, a week earlier. (Note, too, the subtle motivic quotation from the song's melody in the solo's seventh bar.)

As much a triumph for McCartney as STRAWBERRY FIELDS was for Lennon, PENNY LANE fathered a rather smug English pop vogue for brass bands and gruff Northern imagery. However, as the film of *Yellow Submarine* later showed by using similar images in a psychedelic context, the song is every bit as subversively hallucinatory as STRAWBERRY FIELDS. Despite its seeming innocence, there are few more LSD-redolent phrases in The Beatles' output than the line (sung with an ecstatic shiver of grace-notes) in which the Nurse 'feels as if she's in a play' . . . and 'is, anyway'.

18 **All You Need Is Love**
(Lennon–McCartney)

Lennon vocal, harpsichord, banjo; **McCartney** harmony vocal, string bass, bass guitar; **Harrison** harmony vocal, violin, guitar; **Starr** drums; **George Martin** piano; **Sidney Sax, Patrick Halling, Eric Bowie, Jack Holmes** violins; **Rex Morris, Don Honeywill** tenor saxes; **Stanley Woods, David Mason** trumpets; **Evan Watkins, Harry Spain** trombones; **Jack Emblow** accordion; **Mick Jagger, Keith Richards, Marianne Faithfull, Jane Asher, Mike McCartney, Patti Harrison, Eric Clapton, Graham Nash, Keith Moon, Hunter Davies, Gary Leeds** (and others) chorus; **Mike Vickers** conductor.

Recorded: 14 June 1967, Olympic Sound Studios; 19 June 1967, Abbey Road 3; 23–25 June 1967, Abbey Road 1.

Producer: George Martin. Engineers: Eddie Kramer/Geoff Emerick.

UK release: 7 July 1967 (A single/BABY YOU'RE A RICH MAN).

US release: 17 July 1967 (A single/BABY YOU'RE A RICH MAN).

One of The Beatles' less deserving hits, Lennon's ALL YOU NEED IS LOVE owes more of its standing to its local historical associations than to its inspiration which, as with their other immediate post-*Pepper* recordings is desultory. Thrown together for *Our World*, a live TV broadcast linking twenty-four countries by global satellite on 25 June 1967, the song is an inelegant structure in alternating bars of 4/4 and 3/4, capped by a chorus which, like its B-side, BABY YOU'RE A RICH MAN, consists largely of a single note. The order in which the group's recordings of this period were issued concealed the slapdash atmosphere in which they were made and to some extent disguised the sloppiness on show in ALL YOU NEED IS LOVE (a false impression reinforced by the razzmatazz surrounding it). The fact was, though, that The Beatles were now doing wilfully substandard work: paying little attention to musical values and settling for lyric first-thoughts on the principle that everything, however haphazard, meant *something* and if it didn't – so what? Their attention to production, so painstaking during the *Pepper* sessions, had likewise faded. (The engineers at

Olympic, where the backing track was prepared for the TV broadcast, were shocked by the carelessness with which the mixdown was made.)

Drug-sodden laziness was half the problem. In Lennon's case, this was complicated by his oscillating confidence, which had him either wildly overestimating The Beatles ('We're as good as Beethoven') or flatly dismissing them (and art in general) as 'a con'. The rest of the trouble sprang from the ethos of 1967 itself – a passive atmosphere in which anything involving struggle, conflict or difficulty seemed laughably unenlightened. 'It's *easy*' – the half-ingenuous, half-sarcastic refrain of ALL YOU NEED IS LOVE – expressed both this starry-eyed mood and The Beatles' non-evaluative attitude to their music in the dazzling light of LSD. All you had to do was toss a coin, consult the *I Ching*, or read a random paragraph from a newspaper – and then start playing or singing. Anyone could do it, everyone could join in. ('All together now . . .')

The communality of the hippies, like that of the seventeenth-century Nonconformists to whom they looked for precedents, was essentially egalitarian. There was little room in this outlook for 'special' individuals and thus (theoretically, at least) small scope for artistic genius.

Creativity was merely the childlike play of the imagination; we were *all* artists. When Pink Floyd made a TV
appearance to promote their extraordinary second single
'See Emily Play', they were surrounded by a kaftan-clad
crowd of beatific followers resembling fey emissaries
from some future Eden. Shortly afterwards, The Beatles
repeated the trick by performing ALL YOU NEED IS LOVE
knee-deep in garlanded hangers-on, going one better by
having them all sing along.

If the lotus-eating delusion of an egalitarian life of
ease was seductive, its concomitant worship of benign
chance was positively enervating. During the chaotic
sessions for IT'S ALL TOO MUCH, the group filled several
tapes with instrumental ramblings to which they never
later returned, although they were presumably under the
impression that they were doing something worthwhile
at the time. By mid-1967, their enthusiasm for 'random',
which had begun as a sensible instinct for capitalising
on fortuitous mistakes, was starting to degenerate into
a readiness to accept more or less anything, however
daft or irrelevant, as divinely dispensed. Lennon's lyric
for ALL YOU NEED IS LOVE shows the rot setting in: a
shadow of sense discernible behind a cloud of casual
incoherence through which the author's train of thought

glides sleepily backwards. The various musical quotations – collaged onto the backing track by George Martin, working to The Beatles' offhand instructions – are in the same vein, if more to the point, underlining an ambiguity implicit in the orchestra's blowsily derisive rejoinders to the chorus. The presiding spirit of ALL YOU NEED IS LOVE nonetheless has more to do with comfortable self-indulgence than redeeming self-parody.

During the materialistic Eighties, this song's title was the butt of cynics, there being, obviously, any number of additional things needed to sustain life on earth. It should, perhaps, be pointed out that this record was not conceived as a blueprint for a successful career. 'All you need is love' is a transcendental statement, as true on its level as the principle of investment on the level of the stock exchange. In the idealistic perspective of 1967 – the polar opposite of 1987 – its title makes perfect sense.

19 **Hello, Goodbye** *(Lennon–McCartney)*

McCartney double-tracked vocal, backing vocal, piano, bass, bongos, conga; **Lennon** backing vocal, lead guitar, organ; **Harrison** backing vocal, lead guitar; **Starr** drums, maracas, tambourine; **Kenneth Essex, Leo Birnbaum** violas.

Recorded: 2 October 1967, Abbey Road 2; 19 October 1967, Abbey Road 1; 25 October 1967, Abbey Road 2; 2 November 1967, Abbey Road 2.

Producer: George Martin. Engineers: Ken Scott/Geoff Emerick.

UK release: 24 November 1967 (A single/I AM THE WALRUS).

US release: 27 November 1967 (A single/ I AM THE WALRUS).

Recorded after most of the filming for *Magical Mystery Tour* was finished, this blandly catchy McCartney song became The Beatles' first post-Epstein single (much to Lennon's disgust, his I AM THE WALRUS being harmlessly diverted to the B-side). According to group assistant Alistair Taylor, HELLO, GOODBYE began as an exercise in 'random' in which he and McCartney struck alternate notes on a harmonium while playing a word-association game. Childlike lyrics, another by-product of LSD, were then fashionable, McCartney catching a mood set in such 1967 hits as Pink Floyd's 'See Emily Play' and Traffic's 'Hole In My Shoe'. Built on a descending sequence in C, the song's characteristic scalar structure offers a brief touchdown on A flat as its only surprise, yet this, plus its plaintively simple melody and heavily echoed 'Maori finale' – a mistake for 'Hawaiian' (*aloha*) – proved sufficient to secure a big hit. (McCartney took particular care over the bass-line which, like most of those after I WANT TO TELL YOU, was recorded at a later stage on its own track.)

That HELLO, GOODBYE spent seven weeks at No. 1 in the UK, The Beatles' longest stay at the top since [3] SHE LOVES YOU, says more about the sudden decline of the singles chart than the quality of the song itself. Following a period in which Tin Pan Alley and the major labels had lost control to self-reliant groups, a new generation of young female listeners – a segment of the market soon formally categorised as teenyboppers – was

being targeted by old-style manufactured acts master-
minded by traditional writer/producer studio teams.
These, along with pseudo-Beatles like The Monkees and
The Bee Gees, lightweight exploitations of San
Franciscan 'flower-power' and the histrionic bellowing
of proto-'heavy metal' quartet Vanilla Fudge, represented a significant decline in pop's inspiration from its
peak of 1965 to mid-1967. As the divide between pop
and rock widened during the next few years, the brighter
writer-performers would move *en masse* into the album
market, leaving the singles charts to the sort of shallow
'bubblegum' last dominant in the 1959–62 interregnum
between Presley and The Beatles.

20 **Lady Madonna** *(Lennon–McCartney)*

McCartney double-tracked vocal, piano, bass, handclaps;
Lennon backing vocal, lead guitar, handclaps; **Harrison**
backing vocal, lead guitar, handclaps; **Starr** drums, hand-
claps; **Ronnie Scott, Bill Povey** tenor saxes; **Harry Klein,
Bill Jackman** baritone saxes.
  Recorded: 3 February 1968, Abbey Road 3; 6 February
  1968, Abbey Road 1.
  Producer: George Martin. Engineers: Ken Scott/Geoff
  Emerick.
  UK release: 15 March 1968 (A single/THE INNER LIGHT).
  US release: 18 March 1968 (A single/THE INNER LIGHT).

As if to prove himself unaffected by the critical savaging
inflicted on *Magical Mystery Tour*, McCartney bounced
back with another A-side, the second in a row to oust a
rival offering from Lennon. LADY MADONNA, a song
uncontroversially in praise of motherhood, was inspired
by a magazine picture of an African woman suckling her
baby over the caption 'Mountain Madonna'. Styled after

Fats Domino, the music's immediate source was Johnny Parker's boogiewoogie piano line on Humphrey Lyttleton's 'Bad Penny Blues', produced by George Martin in 1956. As such, LADY MADONNA was the first Beatles song (not counting the instrumental FLYING) to use a blues scale since GOOD DAY SUNSHINE – which suggests that McCartney may have been trying to guide the group back to earth after its disembodied LSD phase. If so, the attempt was superficial, for the lyric is tinged with the acid-fuelled unreality that had hung over The Beatles since *Sgt Pepper* (and which was about to shape the ill-fated Apple project). While the words of the verse/chorus hang together, the middle eight wanders off into a string of vaguely associated images, climaxing, on a hymnic suspension, with a pointless allusion to I AM THE WALRUS. Whether this was done to please Lennon or, in a spirit of playfulness, to add another link to an ongoing chain of references, it amounted to wanton – and perilous – self-mythologisation.

Most of the work on LADY MADONNA took place on one day in Studio 3, with a separate late-night session for overdubs. Following his usual practice, McCartney began by taping the piano track plus a guide vocal, accompanied by Starr on brushed snare. (An old microphone was used to obtain the right period piano sound.) After Lennon and Harrison had doubled the riff on fuzz-toned guitars, played together through the same amp, McCartney and Starr added their rhythm section, the rolling bass-line matched by a syncopated bass-drum pattern akin to the swing-beat of the late Eighties. Achieved by limiting, the thunderous low-frequencies of bass and piano were also applied to Starr's kit, in particular the snare sound in the coda. After redoing his Presleyesque vocal, McCartney hired four jazz saxophonists without preparing parts for them, an 'unprofessional' lapse which provoked an audibly exasperated tenor solo from Ronnie Scott. The result was a moderately entertaining let-down after the psychedelic heights of early 1967. Significantly, LADY MADONNA became the first purpose-built Beatles single not to reach No. 1 in America since ELEANOR RIGBY.

21 **Hey Jude** *(Lennon–McCartney)*

McCartney vocal, piano, bass; **Lennon** backing vocal,
acoustic guitar; **Harrison** backing vocal, lead guitar; **Starr**
backing vocal, drums, tambourine; **Uncredited** 10 violins,
3 violas, 3 cellos, 2 double basses, 2 flutes, 2 clarinets, 1
bass clarinet, 1 bassoon, 1 contrabassoon, 4 trumpets, 2
horns, 4 trombones, 1 percussion; **All** backing vocals,
handclaps.

Recorded: 29, 30 July, 1968, Abbey Road 2; 31 July, 1
August 1968, Trident Studios.
Producer: George Martin. Engineers: Ken Scott/Barry
Sheffield.
UK release: 30 August 1968 (A single/REVOLUTION).
US release: 26 August 1968 (A single/REVOLUTION).

McCartney's HEY JUDE was scheduled as a Beatles single
from the moment it was written. Composed while its
author was out for a drive in June 1968, the song was
originally sung as if to Lennon's five-year-old son Julian
('Hey Jules') before McCartney changed it to 'something

a bit more country and western'. Demoing it on piano, he took the tape to Lennon, apologising for the lyric as the first words that had come into his head. His partner would have none of this, dismissing McCartney's embarrassment over the line 'the movement you need is on your shoulder' and declaring HEY JUDE all but finished as it stood. (He later described the song as the best his partner ever wrote.)

After some more work on it on 26 July (probably the harmony on the final verse and the coda melody), the group spent two days trying it out in Abbey Road before deciding they needed an orchestra. So as not to have to repeat the laborious mix-downs entailed by the orchestral recording for A DAY IN THE LIFE, they moved to Soho's Trident Studios, an eight-track which Apple had been using to record acts like Jackie Lomax, Mary Hopkin and James Taylor. Here, on Thursday 1 August, they packed thirty-six highly trained classical musicians into a small room to play four chords over and over again, closing the evening by requesting them to clap and sing along. Persuaded by a double fee, all but one complied.

The monumentality of the orchestral contribution to HEY JUDE – so simple, so surprising – was typical of The Beatles. Their instinct for what worked was rarely sharper, the huge chords suggesting both Jude's personal revelation and, along with the accompanying chorale, a vast communality in which artists and audience joined in swaying to a single rhythm all around the world – an effect which the more casual and ironic [18] ALL YOU NEED IS LOVE had not quite managed to conjure. The first of many such anthem-like singalongs to arise in response to rock's compulsive self-mythologisation, HEY JUDE is a pop/rock hybrid drawing on the best of both idioms. Partly because conceived without an instrument to hand, partly because driven more by feeling than form, its verse/chorus lacks its composer's usual elegant construction, cadencing so often on the tonic that the plain seventh leading to the middle eight seems like the sun coming out. So expressive is the melody, however, that reservations are academic.

The work put in at rehearsal shows in the subtlety of the group's arrangement during the song proper, with bass and piano working off drums and tambourine to give the four-square rhythm a characteristic rolling swing. Faced with a sententious lyric demanding 'interpretation' (and a lot of space in which to do it), McCartney gives a tasteful performance at the bottom of his range, making spare use of gospel-style melismas. His ill-advised pseudo-soul shrieking in the fade-out may be a blemish (as is the curse over a fluffed backing vocal at 2:58), but otherwise HEY JUDE, for all its inordinate length, is a self-evident success. The group's biggest-selling American hit, it held the US No. 1 position for an astonishing nine weeks.

Disputes over who the song was about (the press assumed it was aimed at Dylan) even affected the group. On hearing it, Lennon exclaimed 'It's me!', to which a surprised McCartney countered 'No – it's me! In fact, HEY JUDE strikes a universal note, touching on an archetypal moment in male sexual psychology with a gentle wisdom one might properly call inspired.

22 **Get Back** *(Lennon–McCartney)*

McCartney vocal, bass; **Lennon** harmony vocal, lead
guitar; **Harrison** rhythm guitar; **Starr** drums; **Billy
Preston** electric piano.
  Recorded: 23, 27, 28, 30 January, 5 February 1969,
  Apple Studios.
  Producer: George Martin. Engineer: Glyn Johns.
  UK release: 11 April 1969 (A single/DON'T LET ME
  DOWN).
  US release: 5 May 1969 (A single/DON'T LET ME DOWN).

McCartney's GET BACK, which in April became The
Beatles' nineteenth British single, seems to have origi-
nated as a country blues in the style of Canned Heat's
hits 'On The Road Again' and 'Going Up The Country'.
(The musical links are tenuous, but McCartney liked
both records and busked 'Going Up The Country' in the
studio the night before starting work on GET BACK.) The
title phrase, coined for the abortive concert project,
unfortunately became linked with a studio jam in which,

over a vaguely Caribbean twelve-bar, McCartney improvised a satirical pseudo-calypso about Enoch Powell's claim that immigration into the UK would cause a race war. Preserved on bootlegs as 'Commonwealth Song', this squib had nothing to do with GET BACK itself, being merely part of the general self-conscious fooling about. (On one take, McCartney ad-libbed the entire lyric of GET BACK in Reeperbahn German.)

Recorded on 27 January, the album version of the song lacks the polished mix and glamorous reverb of the single version, recorded on 28 January. It ends with an edit from the rooftop concert in which McCartney thanks Starr's wife Maureen for applauding, while the single, originally several minutes longer, simply fades out. (Lennon claimed that every time McCartney sang the line 'Get back to where you once belonged' he looked meaningfully at Ono.) Made in the same afternoon session as its B-side DON'T LET ME DOWN, the single version of GET BACK showcases The Beatles in smoothly grooving R&B mode, McCartney tossing off the lyric between infectious solos by Lennon and Preston. Deploying fewer chords than any Beatles single since [1] LOVE ME DO, its blend of grace, punch and daftness charmed record buyers enough to shift four million copies worldwide.

23 Let It Be *(Lennon–McCartney)*

McCartney vocal, backing vocal, piano, maracas; **Lennon** bass; **Harrison** backing vocal, lead guitar; **Starr** drums; **Billy Preston** organ, electric piano; **Uncredited** 2 trumpets, 2 trombones, tenor sax, cellos.
 Recorded: 25, 26, 31 January 1969, Apple Studios; 30 April 1969, 4 January 1970, Abbey Road 2.
 Producers: George Martin/Chris Thomas. Engineers: Glyn Johns/Jeff Jarratt/Phil McDonald.
 UK release: 6 March 1970 (A single/YOU KNOW MY NAME [LOOK UP THE NUMBER])
 US release: 11 March 1970 (A single/YOU KNOW MY NAME [LOOK UP THE NUMBER])

Behind the motivator of The Beatles' erratic final years was a hurt and worried man. McCartney threw everything into keeping the group alive, but the price of his endless energy was a lack of instinct for when to leave well alone. Half afraid (as they all were) of Lennon's newly revived sarcasm, he was alternately patronising and insensitive to Harrison and Starr, finding it difficult to say anything to them that didn't cause offence. During summer 1968, when sessions for *The Beatles* were especially hostile, he would lie awake at night in a state of insecurity very different from the light-toned charmer he liked to present in public. In the end, he had an impressive dream in which his dead mother Mary appeared to him and told him not to get so worked up about things – to let them be. Like so many of his experiences, this quickly turned itself into a song.

With its air of supernal consolation and universally understandable lyric (naturally taken by many to refer to the Virgin Mary), LET IT BE has achieved a popularity well out of proportion to its artistic weight. Leaning further to rock than pop, its four-square gospel rhythm, religiose suspensions, and general harmonic monotony offer complacent uplift rather than revelation – [21] HEY JUDE without the musical and emotional release. Lennon made no secret of his aversion to the Catholic sanctimony he heard in this track and during the 31 January session cruelly asked McCartney 'Are we supposed to giggle during the solo?' (He was the moving force behind the mischievous sequencing of the *Let It Be* album, where the song is bracketed between him as a small boy piping 'Now we'd like to do Hark the Angels Come' and a ribald knees-up about a Lime Street whore.)

Harrison added a Leslie-toned guitar solo to take 27 of LET IT BE on 30 April, after which, like most of the January 1969 material, it was left to accumulate dust for the rest of the year. Exhumed at the beginning of 1970, it was given a second, more organised solo with fuzz-tone, some high harmonised backing vocals by McCartney and Harrison, extra drums, maracas, and a George Martin score for brass and cellos. These extra instruments, virtually inaudible on the single version of the track, are mixed higher on the album, where Harrison's second solo is preferred.

24 **The Long And Winding Road**
(Lennon–McCartney)

McCartney vocal, piano; **Lennon** bass; **Starr** drums;
Harrison guitar; **Uncredited** 18 violins, 4 violas, 4 cellos,
harp, 3 trumpets, 3 trombones, 2 guitarists, 14 female
voices.

Recorded: 26, 31 January 1969, 1 April 1970, Abbey
Road 1.

Producers: George Martin/Phil Spector. Engineers: Glyn
Johns/Peter Bown.

UK release: 8 May 1970 (LP: *Let It Be*).

US release: 18 May 1970 (LP: *Let It Be*).

Written on the same day as [23] LET IT BE, THE LONG
AND WINDING ROAD was designed as a standard to be
taken up by mainstream balladeers. (McCartney sent a
demo of it to various candidates, including Cilla Black
and Tom Jones.) Sporadically tried out at the Apple
sessions, it was left undeveloped until Lennon invited
Phil Spector to salvage the January 1969 material a year

later. Spector has been generally slammed for the way
he treated certain tracks, smothering them in orchestra-
tions which obscure the group and contradict the original concept of an 'honest' recording without overdubs.
In this case, while his solution is undeniably tasteless,
he had no choice but to cover the original tape with
something, since it was little more than a run-through
with a good McCartney vocal.

Featuring only its author on piano and Lennon on
bass, the basic take of THE LONG AND WINDING ROAD is
a demo, and a provisional one at that. In particular, it
features some atrocious bass-playing by Lennon, prod-
ding clumsily around as if uncertain of the harmonies
and making many comical mistakes. Whatever else one
may say about his production, Spector's fear in diverting
attention from how badly played the original track is can
only be accounted a success. Yet his overdub session, a
stormy affair on 1 April 1970, took place in Abbey Road's
Studio 1 with McCartney, only minutes away, available
to redo the bass part if asked. Why wasn't he?

In fact, neither McCartney nor George Martin knew
that the 'Get Back' tapes were being prepared for release,
Lennon having taken it upon himself to off-load the task
to Spector after the latter had impressed him with his

production for the Plastic Ono Band's 'Instant Karma' on 27 January. The truth is that The Beatles' creative and financial wranglings had by then torn them apart and they hated each other. Lennon knew that if McCartney had realised THE LONG AND WINDING ROAD was being worked on, he would have stopped the whole *Let It Be* project – or at least taken over the session and produced the song his way (i.e., properly). Lennon's impatient indifference to the maintenance of The Beatles' production standards is, in this case, indefensible. Shortly before his death in 1980, he accused McCartney of having treated Lennon songs with less care than his own – and certainly McCartney's improvisatory bass playing on his partner's tracks often contrasts with the careful lines created for his own material. Yet McCartney left no technical blemish on any Beatles tracks, whoever wrote them. By comparison, Lennon's crude bass playing on THE LONG AND WINDING ROAD, though largely accidental, amounts to sabotage when presented as finished work.

When McCartney heard Spector's patch-up job on his song, he was understandably livid, tried unsuccessfully to block it and, having ensured that his solo album would be released ahead of it, promptly announced that he'd left the group. All this is customarily given as evidence of his high-handed egomania, yet while there was blame on his side, Lennon's behaviour over this track and the whole *Let It Be* affair was appalling. Even the gentlemanly George Martin was scathing about Richard Hewson's orchestration for THE LONG AND WINDING ROAD which, with its mushy wash of sound, flew in the face of the etched, incisive and essentially anti-romantic idiom Martin had painstakingly created for The Beatles during the previous four years. Whether he could have rescued the original track (or would even have considered trying) is another question. Like the tinkling cymbals of Starr's overdub, Hewson's Mantovani strings and Home Service choir are there mainly to fool the listener's ear.

In the event, THE LONG AND WINDING ROAD was so touching in its fatalistic regret, and so perfect as a downbeat finale to The Beatles' career, that it couldn't fail, however badly dressed. Issued in America as the group's last single, it rose to No. 1 as a double A-side with Harrison's FOR YOU BLUE. (I ME MINE would have been a more truthful choice.)

With its heartbreaking suspensions and yearning backward glances from the sad wisdom of the major key to the lost loves and illusions of the minor, THE LONG AND WINDING ROAD is one of the most beautiful things McCartney ever wrote. Its words, too, are among his most poignant, particularly the reproachful lines of the brief four-bar middle section. A shame Lennon didn't listen more generously.

25 **The Ballad Of John And Yoko**
(Lennon–McCartney)

Lennon vocal, lead guitars, acoustic guitar; **McCartney**
harmony vocal, bass, drums, piano, maracas.
Recorded: 14 April 1969, Abbey Road 3.
Producer: George Martin. Engineer: Geoff Emerick.
UK release: 30 May 1969 (B single/OLD BROWN SHOE).
US release: 4 June 1969 (B single/OLD BROWN SHOE).

Among Lennon's assortment of contradictions was a
tension between self-absorption and sympathy for the
underdog. Since this sympathy was based on a projec-
tion of the pessimistic side of his own self-image (John
the orphan, the misfit, the reject), it might be seen as no
different from his self-absorption; yet it *was* distinct in
as much as it motivated some gentleness during times
when distrust, aggression and sarcasm were dominant.
The softness cultivated in him by Yoko Ono had always
been there, seeking expression; indeed, it was awoken
before he met her by LSD. With its beatific imperson-

ality, acid had a profound impact on the outlook of a generation, and Lennon, who took it in enormous quantities, was one of its most influential converts. Among other things, what the drug did for him was to elevate his psychologically conditioned sympathy for the underdog into a universal concern for love and peace which, striking him with the force of conversion, quickly inflated into messianism.

Equally contradictory, Yoko Ono balanced a hard-headed, even heartless percipience with a fey narcissism which, held in check by her intellectual peers in the New York avant-garde scene, ran riot once liberated by Lennon's intuitive and untutored indiscipline. While exchanging comfort and confirmation, the pair brought out the worst in each other, he inadvertently diverting her from the sharp Oriental Dadaism of her early work into a fatuous fugue of legs, bottoms and bags, she encouraging him to believe that orderly meaning was a male hang-up and that the secret of peace was to be sought in pure sensation and guiltless sex. Since she was his intellectual superior, most of the influence ran from her to him; and, since he was her artistic superior, this influence streamed straight into the public domain through his music. Their activities accordingly became

unguardedly naive, their gesture of letting their pants
down on the cover of *Two Virgins* showing how far intel-
ligent people can infantilise themselves by pretending
to believe what at heart they don't. Under the ostensibly
selfless holy foolery they indulged in during 1968–70
was a core of exhibitionistic self-promotion. Behaving as
if they had personally invented peace, they jetted round
the world in first-class seats selling it at third-rate media-
events. This was arrogant as well as silly, and the news
media's derision, of which THE BALLAD OF JOHN AND
YOKO self-righteously complains, was not only inevitable
but, in the main, justified.

Of all the dangerous ideas Ono unloaded on her
spouse around this time, the most damaging was her
belief that all art is about the artist and no one else.
Serving to confirm Lennon's self-absorption, this also
torpedoed his universalism, and it was as a man strug-
gling to resolve this exacerbation of his lifelong
emotional contradictions that he reeled from heroin to
Primal Therapy to Maoism and finally to drink during
the next three years. Otherwise scathingly honest, he
unwittingly put himself into a position in which he was
obliged to defend things that, deep down, he cared
nothing about. Uncompromising as ever, he threw

himself into this trap with total commitment, not only refusing to draw a line between his public and private life but going out of his way to personalise everything that happened in his vicinity, a self-centredness which could hardly avoid occasionally degenerating into paranoia, as THE BALLAD OF JOHN AND YOKO demonstrates. Indeed, so outrageously egocentric is this song that it's difficult to know whether to deplore its vanity or admire its chutzpah in so candidly promoting Self to artistic central place.

Lennon's new autobiographical output soon grew too specific for inclusion in The Beatles' *oeuvre* and by summer 1969 he had done the decent thing and coined an extramural pseudonym: The Plastic Ono Band. Written before this, THE BALLAD OF JOHN AND YOKO fell to The Beatles to deal with and, with Starr booked on *The Magic Christian* and Harrison out of the country, it was down to McCartney to accommodate his partner's urgent need to express himself. Despite his wryness about Lennon's messianic excesses – asked for a sleevenote for *Two Virgins*, McCartney had obliged with 'When two great Saints meet, it is a humbling experience' – he did not hesitate to help, offering him the same unqualified support he had during Lennon's bad trip in

1967 and even mucking in with the writing. Considering the bitterness of the 'Get Back' sessions eight weeks earlier and the fact that the two were now in legal dispute, this is remarkable; yet their friendship was still strong, albeit under strain.

With Lennon's guitar phrases mocking his self-pity, this is a tolerably engaging rocker using a standard period riff, capped with a vintage Beatles sixth. Musically simple, it is enthusiastically played and, like its B-side, mixed with a big bass end. The mostly self-explanatory words caused trouble in America where the reference to crucifixion prompted radio bans and an optimal chart position of 8. (Britain loyally sent the record to No. 1 for a fortnight.)

26 **Something** (*Harrison*)

Harrison double-tracked vocal, lead guitar, handclaps; **McCartney** backing vocals, bass, handclaps; **Lennon** guitar; **Starr** drums, handclaps; **Billy Preston** Hammond organ; **Uncredited** 12 violins, 4 violas, 4 cellos, 1 double bass.

Recorded: 16 April, 2 May 1969, Abbey Road 2; 5 May, Olympic Sound Studios; 11, 16 July, Abbey Road 2; 15 August 1969, Abbey Road 1.

Producers: George Martin/Chris Thomas. Engineers: Jeff Jarratt/Glyn Johns/Phil McDonald/Geoff Emerick.

UK release: 26 September 1969 (LP: *Abbey Road*).

US release: 1 October 1969 (LP: *Abbey Road*).

Harrison and Apple publicist Derek Taylor had a standing joke. Whenever either of them had an idea, they would quip, 'This could be the big one.' SOMETHING, written in mid-1968 on a piano in Abbey Road during a break from work on *The Beatles*, really did become the big one for Harrison. Hurried out as an unscheduled single, it sold only respectably, but it did its business as a vehicle for other artists, eventually acquiring more cover versions than any other Beatles number except [11] YESTERDAY. No less a luminary than Frank Sinatra described SOMETHING, somewhat extravagantly, as 'the greatest love song of the past fifty years'.

According to Harrison, the warmly yielding semitonal sigh of the verse/chorus, its words absent-mindedly taken from the title of a James Taylor song, came easily. The middle eight, on the other hand, had to wait till he found his way up to A major rather than back down to his initial C – and, by then, his lyric inspiration appears to have slackened. (This is the part of Sinatra's version where his maturity is incongrous with what are, in truth, callow sentiments.) Yet the song contains, in its second verse, its author's finest lines – at once deeper and more elegant than almost anything his colleagues ever wrote.

Made, after a false start on 16 April, in five widely separated sessions, SOMETHING was for some while nearly eight minutes long, owing to an extended instrumental appendage, later removed. During this process there was plenty of time for second thoughts, and Starr and McCartney took the opportunity to add to or improve their parts. (Starr's is precisely right; McCartney's, while full of beautiful ideas, is too fussily extemporised.) Harrison, meanwhile, fretted over his guitar solo, in the end redoing it during the session for the album's orchestral overdubs on 15 August, even then remaining unsatisfied with the result. Conceded by Lennon to be the best song on *Abbey Road*, SOMETHING is the acme of Harrison's achievement as a writer. Lacking his usual bitter harmonies, it deploys a key-structure of classical grace and panoramic effect, supported by George Martin's sympathetic viola/cello countermelody and delicate pizzicato violins through the middle eight. If McCartney wasn't jealous, he should have been.

27 **Come Together** *(Lennon–McCartney)*

Lennon vocal, rhythm guitar, lead guitar, handclaps;
McCartney harmony vocal, bass, electric piano; **Harrison**
guitar; **Starr** drums, maracas.
Recorded: 21–23 July, Abbey Road 3; 25, 29, 30, July
1969, Abbey Road 2.
Producer: George Martin. Engineers: Geoff Emerick/Phil
McDonald.
UK release: 26 September 1969 (LP: *Abbey Road*).
US release: 1 October 1969 (LP: *Abbey Road*).

Lennon's return to Abbey Road on 9 July for the start of
work on MAXWELL'S SILVER HAMMER represented his first
contribution to *Abbey Road* since a guitar part on YOU
NEVER GIVE ME YOUR MONEY two months earlier. For
the next fortnight he appears to have done nothing more,
having finished no new songs since [25] THE BALLAD OF
JOHN AND YOKO in April. Instead, most of his energy
seems to have been devoted to importing a bed into the
studio so that his wife, more seriously injured than him

in their Scottish car crash at the end of June, could survey proceedings and lend him moral support. (She had a microphone suspended over her pillow so that she could pipe up if she had anything to say.) Finally, he kick-started himself by messing about with an old Chuck Berry number, 'You Can't Catch Me', unwisely leaving part of Berry's lyric ('Here come old flat-top') in the resulting song.

With its sex-political title, COME TOGETHER constitutes the last of Lennon's espousals of the counterculture while still in the group. Exhortatory/pontifical in the style of his early post-Beatles songs, it pitches a stream of self-confessed 'gobbledygook' at the violent antagonisms of an unenlightened world, implying that the language deployed in such confrontations is a trap and a potential prison. Later taken up by separatist feminists (arguing that the trap and the prison were male creations), this idea was at the cutting edge of alternative politics in late 1969.

Nothing else on *Abbey Road* matches the *Zeitgeist*-catching impact of Lennon's cover-breaking announcement, after two verses of faintly menacing semi-nonsense: 'One thing I can tell you is you got to be free.' The freedom invoked here differs from previous revolutionary freedom in being a liberation from *all* forms and *all* norms, including left-wing ones. In COME TOGETHER, the personal preamble to JULIA is propelled into the public sphere and elevated to the level of (anti-) ideology: a call to unchain the imagination and, by setting language free, loosen the rigidities of political and emotional entrenchment. As such, the song pursues a theme consistent in Lennon's work since I AM THE WALRUS – one partly originating in his LSD-enhanced outsider mentality and partly imbibed from the prevailing countercultural atmosphere of anti-elitism as defined by pundits as diverse as Marshall McLuhan, Arthur Janov, R. D. Laing and Herbert Marcuse.

The archetype of countercultural anti-politics as presented in COME TOGETHER was the head-gaming hippie sage: a bewildering guru/shaman modelled on Timothy Leary, Ken Kesey, Carlos Castaneda's fictional Don Juan, and 'trickster' figures like Mullah Nasruddin and the Zen masters of the Orient. An amalgam of these (with perhaps a dash of cartoonist Robert Crumb's lampoon Mr Natural), the character presented in Lennon's lyric has 'juju eyeball(s)' which suggest the cover of Dr John the Night Tripper's pseudo-voodoo album *Gris-Gris*, released in 1968 and a big hit in Britain's student/underground circles. By verse three, Old Flat-top has metamorphosed into Lennon himself, with asides – 'sideboard(s)' – from Yoko Ono, a reference to her characteristic stance in their interviews. ('Spinal cracker' may refer to the traditional practice of Japanese women of walking on their prone husband's backs to loosen muscular tension and keep the spine supple.)

Again suggesting the influence of Dr John (and, more distantly, that of The Band), the song, a D blues shifting to the relative minor for its chorus, adopts the then-new American 'laid-back' or 'spaced-out' style, in which a stoned laziness of beat and a generally low-profile approach offered a cool proletarian alternative to middle-class psychedelic artifice. The associated drugs in this case were cocaine and heroin (and later the powerful tranquillisers known as quaaludes). Implicit was a passive, observing state of mind perfectly caught in the cloudy white tone of Lennon's double-tracked guitar solo and McCartney's brilliantly idiomatic bass and piano, particularly in his wonderfully poised two-bar envoi to the solo. (Lennon, stingy with his praise, was rightly effusive about his partner's playing here.) A slightly murky mix completes this – for The Beatles – very unusual sound picture.

Enthusiastically received in campus and underground circles, COME TOGETHER is *the* key song of the turn of the decade, isolating a pivotal moment when the free world's coming generation rejected established wisdom, knowledge, ethics and behaviour for a drug-inspired relativism which has since undermined the intellectual foundations of Western culture.

Ian MacDonald

Revolution in the Head
The Beatles' Records and the Sixties

'The most sustainedly brilliant piece of pop criticism and scholarship for years. An astonishing achievement.'

Q Magazine

As dazzling as the decade they dominated, The Beatles almost single-handedly created pop music as we know it. Eloquently giving voice to their time, they quite simply changed the world. This acclaimed book goes back to the heart of the Beatles – their records. Drawing on a unique resource of knowledge and experience to 'read' their 241 tracks – chronologically from their first efforts in 1957 to 'Real Love', their final 'reunion' recording in 1995 – Ian MacDonald has created an engrossing classic of popular criticism.

'A triumph – compelling, seductive, delightful.'

Nick Hornby, *Sunday Times*

£14.00   ISBN 0-7126-6697-4

Also available from Pimlico

Ian MacDonald

The People's Music

In his first book since the acclaimed *Revolution in the Head*, Ian MacDonald takes us on a journey through the music of the sixties and seventies. Starting with one of the most important assessments of Bob Dylan to appear in print for many years, these essays range from the psychedelia of the Beatles and the rebellion of the Rolling Stones to the political activism of John Lennon, the 'dark doings' of David Bowie and the spiritual quest of Nick Drake.

Combining a close reading of the music with a detailed understanding of the times, this collection confirms Ian MacDonald's reputation as one of Britain's most important music journalists. Enlightening and entertaining, *The People's Music* is music writing at its best.

£10.00   ISBN 1-8441-3093-2